YOUNG WRITERS

OVER THE MOON

DEVON

Published in Great Britain in 1997 by
Poetry Now
1-2 Wainman Road, Woodston,
Peterborough, PE2 7BU

All Rights Reserved

Copyright Contributors 1996

HB ISBN 1 86188 176 2
SB ISBN 1 86188 171 1

Foreword

The *Over The Moon* competition was an overwhelming success - over 43,000 entries were received from 8-11 year olds up and down the country, all written on a wide variety of subjects. Reading all these poems has been a painstaking task - but very enjoyable.

Many of the poems were beautifully illustrated. This just emphasises how much time, effort and thought was put into the work. For me, this makes the editing process so much harder.

I hope that *Over The Moon Devon* highlights the diversity of today's young minds. I believe that each of these poems shows a great deal of creativity and imagination. Many of them also express an understanding of the problems, socially and environmentally, that we are all facing.

The poems that follow are all written on different levels, and some are more light-hearted than others. With a considerable variety of subjects and styles, there should be something to appeal to everyone.

Sarah Andrew
Editor

CONTENTS

Ashleigh Primary School

Ellen Penfold	1
Adam Chugg	2
Matthew Pow	2
Christina Somerwill	3
Joseph Winfield	3
Samantha Palethorpe	4
Sian Laughton	4
Charlotte Smith	5
Sarah-Jane Scott	5
Helen Fosh	6
Ross Woolfenden	6
Charlotte Grigg	7
Katie Simpson	7
Emily Langridge	8

Bishopsteignton Primary School

Josie Hooker & Jessica Repton	8
Jayme Nicholson	9
Buddy James	10

Buckfastleigh CP School

Helen Webb	11
Sophie Heike	11
Harriet Blackmore	12
Daniel Smith	13
Jake Lane	13
Philip Taylor	14
Nathan Parsons	15
Sarah Marie Pearce	16
Lee Bright	16
Thomas Clegg	17
Sean Nicholson	17
Lauren Ashton	18
Charlotte Farley	18
Christopher Graham	19
Thomas Richards	19
Melanie Wood	20
Luke Gage	21

Caen Primary School

Briony Mitchell	21
Richard Dixon	22
Daniel Hougton	23

Curledge Street School

Stacey Tolley	23
Emma Dooley	24
Russell Jarman	24
Sophie Williams	25
Zoe Harrison	25
Emily Cryer	26
Jack Lamburn	27

Dartington CE Primary School

Jon Shermon-Byrne	27
Andrew Sandercock	28
Leroy Tucker	29
Jaimie Madeley	29
Kimberley Gillson	30
Maïté Chemin	30
Roddy Bow	31
Robert Cannings	31
Sam Strivens	32
Iona Wilson	32
Hannah Tucker	33
Alexandra Mitchelmore	33
Hayley Veale	34
Luke Carter	35
Ben Gaehl	35
Molly Coldrey	36
Emily Fisher	36
Jesse Tanser	37
Ruben Montes	37
Tom Strivens	38
Rowan Springfield	38
Jonathan Ayling	39
Lydia Frater	39
Victoria Hammond	40
Jonny Rowden	41

Frances Robertson	41
Lamelle Kellett	42
Matthew Luscombe	43
Rebecca Connabeer	43
Ben King	44
Tamsyn Mann	44
Nathan Moynihan	45
Katherine Millman	45
Rose Thomas	46
Alex Whiting	46
Megan Dudley	47
Robert Edwards	48
Edward Coveyduck	48
India Bourne	49
Davey Johnson	49
Freddie Giles	50

Eden Park Junior School

Rebecca Oliver	50
Hannah Lund	51
Michaela Gillard	51
Andrew Chappell	52
Stuart Pointon	52
Adam Dart	53
Ashley Drew	53
Matthew Bradley	54
Debbie Prosser	54
Amy Townsend	55
Jacqueline Hazeldine	55
Charlotte Brady	56
Jared Leaman	56
Christopher Moores	57
Jason Redman	58
Rhys Andrews	59
Adam True	59
Philip Callaghan	60
Samantha Dorling	61
Tara Willis	62
Hannah Foot	62

Denbury CP School

	Alice Bryant	63

Furzeham CP School

	Gary Addison	64
	Martyn Green	64
	Carly George	64
	Sheldon Stokes	65
	Thomas Kowalski	65
	Emma Forster	66
	Fiona Slater	66
	Natasha Farmer	67
	Sophie Howard	67
	Adelaide Follon	68
	Thomas Stokes	68
	Heidi Jones	69
	Claire Porter	69
	Jonathan Watt	70
	Luke Mills	70
	Leanne Giffard	71
	Hayley Hemmings	71
	Hannah Martin	72
	Rachel Shears	72
	Mark Lovell	73
	Stephanie Blower	73
	Victoria Milner	73
	Emily Thorp	74
	Maria Lovell	74
	Christopher Brizio	75
	Charlotte Hamling	75
	Phillip Preston	76
	Faye Vandenberg	76
	Amy Stanford	77
	Adam Anderson	77
	Mark Smith	78
	Andrew Binmore	78
	Jonathan Tozer	79
	Christopher Cornish	79
	Michael Williams	79

Gatehouse Primary School

Nicola Parton	80
Christopher Williams	80
Harriet Mealey	81
Michelle Binmore	81
Ben Strike	81
Louise Thorp	82
Jessica Pickup	82
Emma Caple	83
Joanna Lever	83
Rachel Clark	84
Tom Bellamy	84
Helen O'Brien	84
Emily McLaughlan	85
Ben Chambers	85
Kelly Lomas	85
Michael Ayling	86
Richard Williams	86
Amy Martin	87
Gemma Crawford	87
Leighton Frost	88
Matthew Hogg	88
Adam Willis	89
Annie Connell	89
Matthew Hodgson	90
Louise Hogg	90
Ellen Williams	91
Anthony Banning	91
Jenna Bettinson	92
Ricky North	93
Kerry Shields	93
Matthew Heaton	94
Joanne Osborne	94
Leigh Toney	95
Sarah Brimacombe	95
Laura Jewell	96
Michelle Carter	96

High Bray CP School

Daisy Lang	97
Gessica Boddington	98
Amanda Childs	98
Hannah Robins	99
Emma Crawford	100
Andrew Pink	100
Chloe Jemmison	100
Kelly Lane	101
Joe Doyle	101
Bridie Stevens	102

Newton St Cyres Primary School

Sam Way	103
Emma Hodge	104
Holly Delve	104

Newton Poppleford School

Sarah Stephen	105
Michael McDonald	106
Jodie Peters	106
Victoria Sykes	106
Jessica Tubbs	107
Seline Rodgers	107
Megan Rodgers	107
Mark Broughton	108
Darren Bennett	108
Belinda Rowse	109
Oliver Jones	109
Carly Olliff	110
Amy Jones	110

Pilton Bluecoat Junior School

Simon Ellery	111
Kimberley Large	112
Ryan Saunders	112
Lora Gail Jones	113
Kevin Jordan	113
Sam Lane	114
Helen Rendle	115
Tom Wade	115

Tom Ireland	116
Christopher Kingdon	117
Clare Tanner	117
Karen Ten-Bokkel	118
Lizzie Bunyan	118
Lauren Hole	119
Christopher Williams	119
Jenny Smith	120
Corwin Easey	121
Charlie Falco	121
Natalie Hole	122
Hannah Chapple	122
Bethany Cole	123
Sarah Lake	123
Jason Western	124
Christina Bloor	124
Anthony Birchmore	125
Freya McCaie	125
Daniel Stancombe	126
Sarah Wellington	126

Princetown CP School

Rebecca Graham	127
Rebekka Devey	127
Harry Forbes	128
Emma Garrett	129
Adam Garrett	130
Tammy Pidgeon	130
Adam Court	131
Graham Sargent	131
Charlene O'Neill	132
Robert Finch	132
Mark Easton	133
Wayne Smith	133
Samantha Ingram	134
Elizabeth Cronin	134
Andy Routley	135
Kirsty Masterton	135
Craig Liversidge	136

Rydon CP School

James Hext-Williams	136
Adrian Roderick	136
Charlotte Finch	137
Samuel Smerdon	137
Laura Branfield	138
Lindsey Dunne-Richards	138
Verity Palmer	138
Gemma Beere	139
Laura Rattlidge	139
Sarah Langley	140
Mark Russell	140
Abby Humphreys	141
Richard Matthews	141
Hannah Sherwood	142
Zoe Stokes-Davies	142
Emma Webster	143
Darren Morrell	143
Samantha Thompson	144
Emily Birt	144
Cassie Humphreys	145
Simon Langley	145
Hayley Manning	146
Sarah Shore	146
Simone Mulholland	147
Dayle Ward	147
Craig Harris	148
Laurence Harvey	148
Peter Titt	149
Sophie Seymour	149
Christopher Monk	150
Victoria Elliott & Katie Sneap	150
Ryan R Stansfield	151
Jean-Paul Norris	151
Hannah Bray & Lisa Ward	152
Paul Tomlinson	152
Natasha Sellick & Joanna Higgins	153

Darren Catchpole	153
Tom Teague	154
Liam Mugford	154
Amanda Davis	155
Nicola Thomas	156
Sarah Lowe	157
Tina Sneap	158
Robert Law	159
Daniel Jones	160

St Andrew's Primary School, Buckland Monachorum

Charlotte Simkins	161

St Paul's RC Primary School, St Budeaux

John Beaty	161
Hayley Squires	162
Simon Gilley	162
Leanne Lane	163
Carmen Jarvis	164
Nicola McGerty	164

South Brent Primary School

Emily Hawkins	165
Alice Holland	165
Merin Cox-Davies	166
Rebecca Pitts	166
Laura Pitts	167

Stoke Hill Middle School

Maxine Valpy	167
Adam Bishop	168
David Veron	168
Leanne Rose	169
Nasra Al-Hashmi	170
Andy Bartlett	171
Michael Kevin Crump	171
Emma Ridgeon	172
Sheridan Ingram	173
Amie Ormand	174

The Grove School

Charlotte Stephens	174
Victoria Blake	175

	Lindsay Bishop	176
	Pennie Lamkin	176
Tidcombe Primary School		
	Sarah Harrison	177
	Charlotte Brown	178
	Rosie Lamb	179
	Laura Gratton	180
	Peter Byrom	181
Wembury CP School		
	Kimberly Saunders	182
	Laura Louise Michie	182
	Katrina Rae	183
	Emma Hill	183
	Carly James	184
Woolacombe CP School		
	Katharine Bond	184
	Mark Middlemass	185
	Lucy Cansfield	185
	Kate Kilner	186
Widecombe-In-The-Moor School		
	Christopher Smith	187
	Mark Andrew Whiteside	187
	Amanda Whiteside	188
	George Adaway	188
	Oliver Wakeham	188
	Emma Jones	189
Wolborough C of E Primary School		
	Abigail Faulkner	189
	Kylie Westaway	190
	Gina McDermott	190
	Daniel Bunclark	191
	Laura Flaherty	191
	Katherine Bennett	192
	Richard Ford	192
	Danielle Palmer	193
	Chloe Grove	193
	Emma Westaway	194
	Thomas Raes	194

Woodford Junior School	Billie Bowers	195
	Sam L Faulkner	195
	Angela Gilding	196
	Heather Smith	196
	Mathew Rowlands	197
	Hannah Wickens	198
	Louis Phelps	198
	Liam Clutsam	199
	Chloe Edgeley	199
	Fiona Walton	200
	Amy Blackmore	201
	Ben Herd	201
	Sam Stokoe	202
	Lisa Collins	202
Woodlands Park Primary School	Jacqueline Smith	203
	Kathryn Greer	203
	Kimberley Moses	204
	Jodie Clamp	205
	Lucy Ellis	205
	Nicholas Harris	206
	Richard Lake	206
	Alex Wright	207
	Paula Anderson	208
	Samantha MacDougall	208
	Natalie Roberts	208
	Stephanie Griggs-Trevarthen	209
	Zoe Baines	210
	Ashleigh Goddard	211

MY REFLECTION

I turn on the tap
I see my reflection
Everything I do my reflection does
too.
I pull out the plug
My reflection fades away.

There's my face in the dazzling swimming
pool.
As I swim
My reflection comes too.
My reflection looks weird and wobbly
not like me
How can that be?

I look into a puddle,
I see my face reflecting back
at me.
The sun comes out
it dries up the puddle
There are no more reflections
until another day.

Ellen Penfold (10) Ashleigh Primary School

REFLECTIONS

R eflections refelctions
E verywhere coming from all directions.
F aces faces in the stream
L ittle but big in a funny way.
E verywhere everywhere reflections I see
C onstantly those reflections seem to be me
T hose reflections seem to be me
I see no reflections anymore
O h! It is such a bore
N o more reflections of me in the
S tream I'll come back tomorrow and they'll
    be there again once more.

Adam Chugg (11) Ashleigh Primary School

MY REFLECTIONS

When I look into the drifting pool
I feel all funny and very cool
When I go into the sea
I feel all cold and not me
When I go into the bath
I see a face and have to laugh
But when I go into my room
There's one reflection and that's the
        moon.

Matthew Pow (10) Ashleigh Primary School

A SMASHING POEM TODAY

Swirling and crashing against
the rocks of the Islands
Whooshing past the boats on
Their way fishing
Under the tunnel it's dark
The waves echoing as they crash
Against the walls
The whirling and twisting of the
Whirlpool pouring
All bits of rubbish together
Crashing and splashing as the
Waves avoid the boats and the rocks
Once again.

Christina Somerwill (11) Ashleigh Primary School

REFLECTIONS

Reflections looking up at me
Reflections moving wildly
I look in the water and what
do I see?
I look in the water and I see
Me.
I look again and the reflection is
gone.
It's all gone away
So I must go and play
The ocean is there looking at me
I find it incredibly wild the
same as the sea.

Joseph Winfield (10) Ashleigh Primary School

THE WHALE

The whale
Twisting and splashing
Crashing making waves, swirling
and swaying side to side
Around the whale whirling and
Twirling, dripping and crashing
Curling and flowing as it goes past.
On the whale it's spotted and
Dotted, little lines twisting
Can you see the whale
With an open
Mouth.

Samantha Palethorpe (11) Ashleigh Primary School

REFLECTIONS

Reflections reflections can be wiggly, whirly
twirly, wobbly in the rushing stream
Can be of rocks, of you, of the clouds
Whatever the weather.
Birds looking down at themselves in the still
blue lake thinking I love this place especially
the sea where else would you see how
pretty I really am.
A little frog jumps in the reedy pond, so he
makes a big splash, every reflection shakes.

Sian Laughton (10) Ashleigh Primary School

REFLECTIONS

I looked in the cold still river
There I saw my reflection
Staring back at me
She was drifting from side to
side.
I went to touch her . . .
Spots of her started to go,
Big waves were crashing over her
Then she disappeared
Back into the cold river.

Charlotte Smith (10) Ashleigh Primary School

REFLECTIONS

When I look into the water, what do I see
One of my reflections staring back at me.
Flowing and blowing the water spins around
Even though it rushes it doesn't make a sound.

When I walk along the river what do I see
The sun's reflection how beautiful it can be
When it suddenly gets darker the reflections fade away,
When the reflections have gone it's the end of the day.

When I look into the pond what do I see,
I see a reflection of a bush and a tree.
The still pond is only resting there,
It's not moving it's just bare.

Sarah-Jane Scott (10) Ashleigh Primary School

AS THE WAVES GATHER

As the waves gather
                bigger and bigger
The higher it gets
                The closer it comes
Splashing and crashing over the rocks
Here comes the others gathering
            again.

Helen Fosh (11) Ashleigh Primary School

REFLECTIONS

Reflections in the water
Reflections drift around
Reflections flow gently in rivers
Reflections safe and sound.

Reflections shifting down a brook
Reflections waiting to be took
Reflections resting on the sea
Reflections slowly waiting for me,

Reflections happen everywhere
Reflections happen I don't care
Reflections starting in a stream
Reflections smooth, smooth like cream.

Ross Woolfenden (10) Ashleigh Primary School

THE REFLECTIONS IN MY POND

As I look into the cold, calm pond
I see a reflection it's me I can see.

I can see reflection of the trees, flowers
and my cat Fizz
Their reflections I can see, in my cold, calm pond.

It's started to rain
The reflections in the pond are going all fuzzy.

It's all wobbly as it started getting worse
The cold, calm pond is not calm anymore, it's
splashing and crashing.

It's like sea waves, rough and hard as
it can get.

Charlotte Grigg (10) Ashleigh Primary School

REFLECTIONS

They're always here
They're there to be seen
No-one cares
But you don't know where they've been.

In shimmering water
There I see
My reflection in the water
Looking back at me.

In the water
On the side of a car
As I look in the mirror
There you are.

Katie Simpson (11) Ashleigh Primary School

UNTITLED

As I look at
      my picture
I can see
An archway of a dark tunnel
A red clown's happy smile
      and then
A dirty old boot.
All the things I can see
A twisting and turning a bit like
Me!

Emily Langridge (11) Ashleigh Primary School

THE OAK TREE

The oak tree sways, its branches waving in the wind.
Bees weave their way in and out of the dense forest of leaves.
Tall branches reach for the sky, showing their display of colour.
Ripe acorns drop softly to the ground, tumbling slowly through the air.
Birds dance and play around their home, twittering and cheeping till
                                                                                         day is done.
The sun sets over the oak tree, spreading its glow over the world.

The wind whistles through the gnarled branches.
The moon shines over the tree, making its leaves glisten and twinkle
                                                                                         like jewels.
The owl swoops out of its hollow, hooting and cooing with laughter.
The fox arrives with his prey and settles underneath the oak for his meal.
The grumpy badger strolls out of his set, eyeing the fox's prey - his
                                                                                         mouth watering.
The oak tree sighs - its life will soon be over; pray that the animals will
                                                                                        live on after its death.

Josie Hooker & Jessica Repton (10 & 11) Bishopsteignton Primary School

THIS IS NOT A POEM

I'm sat here feeling tired and bored,
I'm sat here feeling lonely and ignored,
This is not a poem!

My mum keeps nagging me,
The cat's scratching me,
This is not a poem!

My brother is banging, crash, wallop,
The dog walked into the wall, silly twallop,
This is not a poem!

My dad's calling me,
The cat's still scratching me,
This is not a poem!

Dad's calling me,
I have to go to tea,
This is not a poem!

My dad's dragging me from my seat,
'What kept you?' he asked pulling me to my feet,
'Oh,' I said 'I was just writing a poem!'

Jayme Nicholson (11) Bishopsteignton Primary School

JACKO THE CLOWN

Jacko the clown went to town juggling on a bicycle.
Along came a dog,
And knocked Jacko into a bog.
As for a clown Jacko was feeling
                        very
                            down.

Jacko the clown went to town to get a sweet.
Down came a pile of meat,
And landed on Jacko's feet.
As for a clown Jacko was feeling
                        very
                          very
                            down.

Jacko the clown went to town to get a new bicycle.
Down came an icicle and turned Jacko's bicycle
into a tricycle.
As for a clown Jacko was feeling
                        very
                          very
                            very
                                down.

Jacko the clown went to the park and went on the slide.
He slipped off into a puddle.
As for a clown this didn't rhyme,
So it's a totally different matter.

Buddy James (10) Bishopsteignton Primary School

SCHOOL

Children running everywhere
Classes full, none are bare
Assemblies taken in the hall
Waiting for the class lunch call
Outdoor lessons on the grass
Teachers saying 'Quiet class'
PE lessons with ball and bat.
Someone's brought in an old pet cat!
I go to this school every day
and enjoy it, come what may.

Helen Webb (10) Buckfastleigh CP School

WINTER SNOWFLAKES

One winter's day
I looked out of my window
And what did I see?
I saw floating snowflakes
Twisting and turning down to the
Ground
They looked like feathers
Falling to the ground
The snow white flakes
Like big fluffy clouds up in the sky
When I went outside
What fun I had catching the snow.

Sophie Heike (7) Buckfastleigh CP School

BUMBLE BEE

I've found a bumble bee
I wonder if mum will be proud of me
It doesn't even sting me

Into the kitchen with my bumble bee
Look, mum! Look, mum! Can't you see
I've found a bumble bee

It doesn't even sting me
Oh, you silly boy, Charles
It will, Charles

Yes, it will sting you
Oh no, it won't mum
Oh yes, it will, Charles

Oh no, it . . .
Ow! You're right, mum
I feel all hot

And tight, mum
It stung my little finger on the right
Mum.

Harriet Blackmore (7) Buckfastleigh CP School

FOOTBALL

I love football it makes me feel great
Playing alongside my mates
Running down the wing is my thing
Scoring goals to make us win.

On the coach here we go
On the way to Wem-ber-ley
Twin towers beckon
Is getting closer and closer
On the way to Wem-ber-ley
I scored the winning goal
Which made me feel
On top of the world!
The crowd went wild!
And I went up the Wem-ber-ley steps to get the
Cup.

Daniel Smith (11) Buckfastleigh CP School

ENGLAND V GERMANY

The match starts, the crowd roar
I think Germany are playing very poor
England score in the first three minutes
Shearer hits and the crowd goes wild.

The German team have kicked it out
It's a corner!
Gascoigne crosses it for Shearer
Shearer misses by about an inch
Germany scores, they race about
The score is now 1 all
The pressure is on, without a doubt!

Jake Lane (10) Buckfastleigh CP School

THE MOON IS LIKE

The moon
    is like
        a wedge of mouse nibbled Edam cheese
          in a larder at the rear of a house

The moon
    is like
        a bruised banana lying in a fruit bowl
          on top of a mahogany table top

The moon
    is like
        a miserable face of a corpse in a coffin
          about to be buried in the gloomy graveyard

The moon
    is like
        a silver croissant in the sky which shines over England
          Frightened because the golden sun devours it at dawn

The moon
    is like
        a lantern hanging from thin air
          even if you can't see it it's still there.

Philip Taylor (11) Buckfastleigh CP School

THE SUN IS LIKE

The sun
      is like
          a burning fire ball in a
          big gun in the sky.

The sun
      is like
          a tree on fire and bonfire
          alight

The sun
      is like
          a flame of fire in a stove
          like an oven cooking.

The sun
      is like
          a torch on fire made
          from a lighter.

The sun
      is like
          a big star in the universe
          a comet going fast.

Nathan Parsons (10) Buckfastleigh CP School

THE EAGLE

The eagle flying high, high in the sky
Swooping and hovering, looking for its prey
It sees a rat
it dives deep and in its claws is the poor little rat
The rat bit the eagle and the eagle dropped the rat
The eagle's leg was red and swollen
An hour later the eagle floated down to the ground
and lay there
flat

Sarah Marie Pearce (10) Buckfastleigh CP School

MY NANNY'S CAT

My nanny's cat is black and white
It makes a noise at teatime
Me and my sister feed the cat,
With chunky turkey slices.

My nanny's cat is round and fluffy,
She comes in and out all day.
Me and my sister play with her,
We pretend we are cats as well.

My nanny's cat has a very long tail
She looks like a panda bear.
She washes her face with her tongue and paws,
And sleeps in her very own bed.

Lee Bright (8) Buckfastleigh CP School

RAINDROPS

The raindrops are falling,
The raindrops are dropping,
The raindrops are splashing
The raindrops are splishing
The raindrops are dribbling
Down the *windowpane.*

Thomas Clegg (7) Buckfastleigh CP School

SNOW

Snow, snow, snow
Oh that fun snow!
So light and fluffy
You are so
Ccccold!
Snow, snow how old are you?
Some people told me the answer.
But I don't think it is true
So please, oh please
Answer my question.

Okay, okay, okay
I am 100 million years old!
Thank you snow, snow
You kind snow
I like you so much
I want you to stay.

Sean Nicholson (8) Buckfastleigh CP School

AT THE SEASIDE

The waves come in, the waves come out.
The sand is smooth between your toes.
The sun's very hot, you must put on
cream.
Yes you must.

The sea is cool, very cool.
'Why don't you go for a splash?'
'Why, I'm hungry. Let's have a picnic.'
Oh! The sandwiches are full of sand.

Lauren Ashton (7) Buckfastleigh CP School

THE TEDDY BEAR

The teddy bear, the teddy bear,
Sits on your shelf.

The teddy bear, the teddy bear,
Sleeps in your bed.

The teddy bear, the teddy bear,
Is nice and soft.

The teddy bear, the teddy bear,
Feels nice and cuddly.

The teddy bear, the teddy bear,
Belongs to *me*.

Charlotte Farley (7) Buckfastleigh CP School

RABBITS

Rabbits are nice
Rabbits can jump
Rabbits are cuddly
Rabbits are furry
Rabbits eat carrots
Rabbits are funny
Rabbits are scared
Rabbits have long ears
Rabbits have four legs
Rabbits have paws
This rabbit is mine but it is not yours.

Christopher Graham (7) Buckfastleigh CP School

MY DINOSAUR

Enormous
Scaly
Small pawed
Massive feet
Three-toed
Dangerous
String legged
Lumpy skulled
Blue backed
Yellow spotted
Pachycephalosaurus

Thomas Richards (9) Buckfastleigh CP School

THE PLAYGROUND

Now the playground is bare, it is deserted and dull
Then you hear thud, thud, thud and before you know it the playground is happy, colourful and loud.

Now the birds and the leaves and the litter take over the playground
Then a cloud bursts and it starts to rain
All the animals run away and the playground is left wet.

Then the sun comes out but the wind is strong
The crisp packets are getting dragged along the floor
A spider's web has just been broken.

Crab apples are falling off trees and rolling around on the floor.

A tin can is making a clattering noise on the ground
Then the children come out with their coats on and again the playground is full of colour and laughter.

Melanie Wood (11) Buckfastleigh CP School

A FARM POEM

Farms have tractors,
Farms have cows.
Farms have bullocks,
Farms have pigs.
Farms have horses,
Farms have sheepdogs.
Have you ever milked a cow?
I have.

Luke Gage (7) Buckfastleigh CP School

CLICK, CLICK, CLICK

A train goes along a railway,
Click, click, click.

With its people on it
Click, click, click.

It loves to go along the railway,
Click, click, click.

It goes to America
It goes to France,
And goes to islands far away.

Briony Mitchell (7) Buckfastleigh CP School

NOW AND THEN

Now

The playground is boring
and bare, quiet, deserted
and no-one to care. A
bird pecks at a crisp

Then

The bell rings, children
rush out and kick a ball
about, noisy games are
being played. A teacher
tells someone off for
kicking. Then the bell
rings

Now

The playground is boring
and bare, quiet, deserted,
no-one to care.

Richard Dixon (11) Buckfastleigh CP School

RED

Blood dripping from a whale
Stabbed by a harpoon.
The whale is dead now!
The blood is overtaking the area
as it spreads.
Everything is becoming red
and
everything is choked
as the blood moves with the
current.

Daniel Hougton (11) Buckfastleigh CP School

OUR PLAYGROUND

Skip
Jump
Hop
Stamp
Play polo
Shout polo
I won, I won
you did not
play again
play again
see who wins
see who wins.

Stacey Tolley (8) Caen Primary School

OUR GAME CALLED TRIO

I know a playground in the school
we play a game called *Trio*
it's fun and cool and it's called *Trio*
we run and run and it's called *Trio*
you are it, you are it and it's called
Trio
one to ten, one to ten and it's called
Trio
and the game is called *Trio*.

Emma Dooley (9) Caen Primary School

COUNTRY

On a cold winter's evening
you hear the wind blowing through the trees,
walking round the dark shadowy bushes,
feeling the cold damp mist by the river
hearing the wind whistling round the branches.
Sheep in the fields beyond,
hear the distant howls of wolves,
And then the birds start to wake up
for the sun has just appeared over the horizon.

Russell Jarman (11) Caen Primary School

SOMETIMES

The sea is like blue silk in the wind sometimes,
I think it's magic sometimes,
I hear it whisper to me in a soft gentle voice,
Sometimes I sit and think to myself
that mighty sea is so strong yet so gentle and calm,
or sometimes I would stand at the lighthouse and
feel the wind blowing sharp against me like Jack Frost
nipping at my face . . . sometimes.

Sophie Williams (10) Caen Primary School

THE FUTURE FOR US

What will the future bring for me?
I don't know we'll have to see.
Maybe I'll go to college and pass.
Maybe I won't perhaps I'll come last.

What will the future bring for you?
You could have a child or maybe two.
What about a job, a singer, a dancer,
a doctor, a vet.
Nobody knows you can't tell yet.

Zoe Harrison (10) Caen Primary School

TUCK SHOP

Miss Miss
can I have this?
Miss Miss
I want this
20p 30p 40p
Miss Miss
I want this
Then one day the tuck shop shut,
The children were all sad
Then the children really wished
That they hadn't been so bad.
No more chocolate no more coke
No more melted bars to poke
No more teachers to ignore
No more money at the door
So we decided to open it by ourselves
and put the cans back on the shelves
We got the teachers to ignore
and we'd pay our money at the door
and these are all the sounds we hear
round the tuck shop far and near
Miss Miss, can I have this?
Stop Stop Stop Stop
The tuck shop's just about to *shut!*

Emily Cryer (10) Caen Primary School

SCHOOL

School you work
School you have fun
School you make friends
School you have happy times with your friends
And when the bell rings you all run home!

Playtime we have fun
Playtime we play football
Playtime we have our apples
Playtime we play games with our friends
And when the bell rings we all go in and work!

Jack Lamburn (8) Caen Primary School

THE SEASONS

I am the season where the
snow will glow and the
temperature's low.

I am the season where the
flowers grow where the grass
will show and no winds will
blow.

I am the season where the sun
shines at night and evenings
are long and mornings are
bright.

I am the season where
the leaves will drop and
the flowers fall and
growing will stop.

Jon Shermon-Byrne (11) Curledge Street School

TAKE THAT

Take me away from this horrible
place
I can't stand the sight of my aunty's
face
As I walked in the door, urgh! A
big sloppy kiss
I'm bored take me away I've had
enough!

I broke the teapot and squashed
the cake
I think it was a big mistake
I looked at my aunty her face
was bright red
I think she wanted to chop off
my head.

I strangled the dog, it got on my
nerves
And I think it got what it really
deserved
My stupid aunty called me a brat
so I kicked the TV and said
     Take That!

Andrew Sandercock (11) Curledge Street School

THE EAGLE

An eagle is a bird of prey,
Look there's one heading this way.
It sees a rabbit over there,
The rabbit can't go anywhere
Not much was said,
The rabbit's dead,
The eagle's gone back so his
young can be fed.

Leroy Tucker (11) Curledge Street School

DAY AND NIGHT

As the sun slips down
and says good night
the moon rises up
and shines its light

The gleaming stars
high above my head
tell all small children
it's time for bed

And when the moon
is sinking down
up comes the sun
with a golden crown.

Jaimie Madeley (10) Curledge Street School

THE SEASONS

I am the season when rivers
flow and flowers grow.

I am the season when ice-cream
comes and we all have fun.

I am the season when leaves fall
and we rake them all.

I am the season when icy snow
falls and Jack Frost calls.

Kimberley Gillson (11) Curledge Street School

THE BLACK CAT

Our next door neighbour's cat
is black with big soft
velvet ears.

Her golden eyes shine so bright
at night
When we all go to bed.

Her tiny nose with see through whiskers
and her bright pink tongue.

Her long furry tail hangs along
behind her.

The sharp white claws she scratches
you with if you hurt her.

I think that's all
I can tell you about her.

Maïté Chemin (10) Dartington CE Primary School

THE GREAT ROBBERY

The shadow of a creepy man appears around the back!
He creeps straight through the window without a tiny crack!
He walks about very slowly holding a big sack!
He finds what he is looking for and puts it in his sack!
He swings his sack onto his back!
He tiptoes to the window and runs off down the track!
        So watch out
        For one day
        He may be
        Back!

Roddy Bow (10) Dartington CE Primary School

WE DIE WITHOUT TREES

Trees give us oxygen
Oxygen we need
If we had no oxygen
We could not breathe!

Trees give us wood
Wood does us good
We could use wood
For a lot more things
I think we should!

We must plant trees
I think we should
Or we could not breathe
And we'd have no wood!

Robert Cannings (9) Dartington CE Primary School

AT MIDNIGHT

The vampire slowly flew out of his tomb,
His shadow like a pathway to doom,
Flying swiftly through the wind,
Prepared to give no mecy this woebegotten night,
His eyes like pools of fire,
His skin icy white,
He passes an open window,
The silent sleeping form of his victims,
The irresistible look of the sleeping boy,
The vampire flew over to his prey,
His fangs sank into the innocent victim's
Neck he took his fill and flew away,
Out into the cold and still night
Leaving his victim behind.

Sam Strivens (10) Dartington CE Primary School

SLAPTON

Lapping against the pebbly shingle,
Its mighty power ready to leap,
Slowly, slowly,
Gaining, gaining,
Washing up upon the shore,
Hidden beneath its silent beauty,
The angry yell of mighty power,
On the top it smiles with glee,
Underneath it grins a smile of evil terror
of mighty power.

Iona Wilson (11) Dartington CE Primary School

IN THE CLASSROOM

'I've spilt my cartridge' shouts someone.
'Quick here's a cloth' shouts another.
'She's coming' shouts someone else
'I know, put your book over it'
'What's the fuss about!'
'Mrs Broom quick!'
'Nothing to worry about' shouts Peter
'Everything's fine.'
'Good now move your book and let me
sit down!'
'No Miss please go and sit on your own
chair it will be a lot more comfortable'
'No let me sit down!'
Splat! 'I did warn you Miss!'

Hannah Tucker (10) Dartington CE Primary School

SLAPTON SEAS IN 1944

The sea hits the shore like a bomb
pushing the pebbles around, every time
a wave comes in.
They bring new pebbles to the shore
and when the waves go out
they take the old pebbles with them.

The training soldier's bodies lie at the
bottom of the sea.
As they went down you could hear
Screams of help and n-o-o-o everywhere.
Where a body went down a trail of blood
Leading to where the body had gone
followed it.

Alexandra Mitchelmore (11) Dartington CE Primary School

MYSTERIOUS SEA

The sea is a mystery to me
The waves crash against the shore
Like hands
Pulling stones and pebbles in.
Sometimes calm
Sometimes rough.
The sea has claimed lives that once
lived.
How many people are in the
Deep
Dark
Blue
Sea?
Nobody knows how many lives have been
taken
Hands pulling them further and further
out into the sea
Feeling life trickle
away from the heart.
People gasping for breath
Now they belong to the sea,
and will forever more.
They have been pulled into death
and cannot get out.
You watch the sea, thinking,
 what really lies at the bottom
Watching the light shades glittering in the sun
and the dark shades lurking in the deep.

Hayley Veale (11) Dartington CE Primary School

SEA AND WAR!

Seagulls squealing screaming like soldiers in the water.
Waves hitting the shore, birds covered in black oil.
People's rustling feet on the shore.
Box ammo sacks thrown onto the places and yellow poppies.
Reeds blowing in the smog flames out at sea.

Luke Carter (10) Dartington CE Primary School

ANSWER THAT PHONE!

'Bring, bring'. That's the phone,
Probably the insurance rung up to have a moan.
Oh well, worth a try,
I pick up the phone, admitting a sigh.
But to my surprise, it's Aunty Sue,
Saying, 'Wouldn't want to come out to the lake for a
picnic today, would you?'
'Yes, yes of course I would,
And my mum, dad and sister should.'
We get in the car, and go to our Aunt's
(which isn't far.)
We get there at 10.25,
And pull into Sue's drive.
When we were on the picnic,
I was very, very glad,
that I'd done what I had,
And instead of having a moan,
I'd picked up the phone.

Ben Gaehl (10) Dartington CE Primary School

AUTUMN SEA

Whitey silver sea
Throwing your waves at me
Moon pulling the tide around
Soft white sand covered the ground
Cool and peaceful the autumn breeze
Fluttering over the soft seas
Shadow of the night closing in
On an autumn's evening beach.

Molly Coldrey (10) Dartington CE Primary School

MIRK WOOD

Misty, cold and dark,
Still, quiet and scary.

Coloured eyes
Staring at us
From every direction.

Shadows all around,
Scaring me even more.

The trees are old.
They look as if they are about to fall.
They are lifeless.

It is mystical, musty, magical and mysterious.
I feel shivery,
scared,
spooked.

Emily Fisher (10) Dartington CE Primary School

AUTUMN

The piles of leaves
    the river has brought them
All these colours are just so awesome.

The greeny nettles and ferns
The sun never burns.

The cold, cloudless sky
That caught my eye.

The salmon are leaping
They are not sleeping.

All the trees and the lazy bees
    the bees look drunk
As they slowly slunk up someone's trousers.

The Autumn is here
    the winter is near
And the sky is so clear.

Jesse Tanser (10) Dartington CE Primary School

MY DAD'S BELLY

He drinks a lot of beer, a gallon a day.
In front of the telly every day, his big belly
Grows with food.
It provides a soft landing when I fall.
I jump up and down, like on a trampoline,
I love to jump on my dad's belly.

Ruben Montes (10) Dartington CE Primary School

DEATH!

Death is behind you all the way,
To your very last minute
From your very first day,
It sees your every move,
Whether you're near or far,
You cannot hide anywhere on earth,
Death creeps up on you faster and faster,
Until one day everything tingles,
Then you feel nothing,
You hear nothing,
You see nothing,
You have had your time on the side of
The living,
You will now sleep forever . . .

Tom Strivens (11) Dartington CE Primary School

FRIEND

Hesitant - just like a cat
When it's hunting,
Slow - and always stopping.
He likes to wear black -
Like a black cat,
Good for hunting.
He has white shoes -
Like a cat with white paws,
And quiet for hunting.
He has bright eyes -
Not as bright as a cat,
But all the better for hunting.
He has short hair -
Like a short-haired cat,
Less noise,
For hunting.

Rowan Springfield (11) Dartington CE Primary School

THE BLACK HOLE

The giant star's about to burst,
A super-nova of the worst
kind possible,
It will turn into a black hole, so it will be able
to suck in everything, including light,
and rock and planets, and with its massive might,
it can suck in stars,
And crush them into a tiny space
swirling round the hole in an interstellar race.

Jonathan Ayling (11) Dartington CE Primary School

THE HOBBIT AND THE DRAGON

Sleek, sly, sharp eye,
Long, thin, tends to lie.

>Sneaky, scaly, veiny, still,
>Makes a hobbit feel quite ill.

Bloodthirsty creature waits in the depths
Till some foolish hobbit doesn't watch where it steps.

>It bites and snarls and waves its tail,
>Now poor little hobbit is weak and frail.

The fight goes on, the hobbit wins,
He waves his sword with one last swing.

>The hobbit returns to all his friends,
>And falls asleep inside Bag End.

Lydia Frater (11) Dartington CE Primary School

TACKY TRAINERS

I got my new trainers yesterday,
Please don't laugh,
They were only £3.99,
Please don't laugh!
Their make is called *Thunder*
They make me run real fast,
I got my new trainers yesterday,
Please don't laugh.

I took my dog for a walk yesterday
In my new trainers,
The dog did a poo on the floor
And my trainers walked straight past!

We did PE yesterday
I wore my new trainers
I jumped onto the monkey bars,
My trainers got me really far,
In fact I jumped higher than the bars
And got stuck to the ceiling
I hung there for days on end,
Until I finally fell
I'm going to sue the make of *Thunder*
My trainers just popped!

Victoria Hammond (11) Dartington CE Primary School

LITTLE MOUSE

There was a little mouse
who lived in a little house,
and in that little house
there was a little room.
In that little room
there was a bit of gloom.
Outside the little room
there was a little kitchen,
but it wasn't old enough to have any lichen.

Jonny Rowden (10) Dartington CE Primary School

THE PEOPLE OF THE SEA

Screams coming from deep
beneath the water's level.
The last few bubbles came up to
the water's surface.
Then, silence the whole ocean
is quiet and deserted.
Swishing swashing as the water
reaches the shoreline.
As I look down into the deep
Dead sea I can sense hundreds
of brave soldiers lying there
at the bottom of the deep deserted sea.
I can sense the sadness and
terror of the war in their eyes.
Then, every few minutes I hear
haunting echoing shouts of the
people who gave up their
lives, for us,
Just lying there silent and still.

Frances Robertson (11) Dartington CE Primary School

THE THING

The moonlight streaming through the palm trees,
Causing the thing to move into the shadows
For fear of the lake's reflection.
For fear of something,
somebody,
seeing.
For fear of the night:
the moon,
the trees,
the stars.

With their beauty
he was evil,
With their light
he was dark,
With their smiles
he was gloomy,
With their sparkle,
he was weak,
With their wisdom
he was foolish,
With their truth
he was fake.

The truth, the light,
The wisdom, the smiles,
The sparkle, all deep down inside him,
But the evil comes first -
The first and the last!

Lamelle Kellett (10) Dartington CE Primary School

MIRK WOOD

Creepy, quiet, still and dead,
Cold and ancient, stale and still.
Trees old and leaves rotting,
Shadows, black, lifeless, distorting.
Never ending, trapped, dreary,
Shadows creeping, dying.
Watching, waiting, cold, frightened.
Foggy, lifeless, damp.

Matthew Luscombe (11) Dartington CE Primary School

THE GREBE

He's at it again
The pedal-boat monster,
Always after me!
He's coming up close!
Quick I better move.

His body is wide and paddles along,
Coming, coming, coming, towards me,
I try to lose the great big thing,
But still he trudges along.

I wonder
Is the pedal-boat monster ever scared
Of anything!

Even though I'm swift, careful,
Always on the go,
He too is swift more careful
And free.

Rebecca Connabeer (11) Dartington CE Primary School

THE LIFE BOAT

The crashing of the waves on the seashore.
The bobbing boat so calm.
Then crash the boat splinters on the rocks.
The crew stand screaming.
It's a job for the lifeboat crew
Then through the storm the lifeboat comes
Then in seconds the men are safe.

Ben King (11) Dartington CE Primary School

THE SEA KNOWS

Up, down
Up, down
How many waves does the sea have?
How much blue is there in the sea?
All these things are mysteries to me
Only the sea knows . . .

How many rings does a limpet have?
Only the sea knows.
How many pebbles are there in the sea?
Only the sea knows.
How much seaweed grows?
Only the sea knows.

These are mysteries to
Me, you
But not the sea
The sea knows everything . . .
Even
Me!

Tamsyn Mann (10) Dartington CE Primary School

THE WORLD AND HOW IT IS

The world is a place with evergreen trees
with busy flies and buzzing bees,
in the night it is dark
and the light is in day,
and the children from school come out to play.

The world has big cars,
and oil tankers,
that spill all their oil
and kill all the birds,
the people do try to clean it up;
and the green peace men go tut tut tut.

The government make a big big fuss
whether or not to ban beer, pubs or drugs.
The people cry 'We do not want this'
but the government rule
and that's all it is.

The countries have wars,
silly it is,
but that's what they do
and kill lots of people,
and that's the world and that's how it is.

Nathan Moynihan (11) Dartington CE Primary School

THE SEA

Dead bodies drift
with the crushing of the waves,
But the gentle coast in its warm calm way
Seems loving but the bad things hide away,
The old bullets and the blood in the waves,
When it beats on the shore with the
Memories aboard think of the things it has seen.

Katherine Millman (11) Dartington CE Primary School

SCARLET SUNSET

After sunset,
bloodshot red,
fluffy clouds,
blushing around the cherry sun,
Clouds breathing around the ruby display,
sinking lower away from your eyes,
distinguished,
from the sky,
Leaving red bleached clouds
until the over shaded black shadow pulls over.

Rose Thomas (10) Dartington CE Primary School

THE UNICORN

As it gallops restlessly on
Its mane and tail glowing
Its hooves and eyes and coat is glowing.
Its long silken tail touches the ground
It gallops on without a sound.
It stands by the water cold and clear
It stops by the moon on the hill to rear.
Its horn has a magic gleam at the end
Power and magic are its only friend.
It takes off to sail across the sky
If man is to touch it it must die.
Man is its only enemy
It must be kind to the wind to be free,
But because it wasn't it is just a memory.

Alex Whiting (10) Dartington CE Primary School

THE SEA ON TRIAL

The sea is strange
The sea is wild
It can be rough
It can be mild

The wave breaks
The sea gets rough
Another person's drowning
The sea is tough

She is so tired
She tries to fight
She can see up through the water
A glimpse of light

She doesn't have a chance
To survive anymore
The sea has crowded her
What's it for?

The sea is guilty
Now she's dead
She lies at the bottom
On the seabed.

Megan Dudley (11) Dartington CE Primary School

SEA POEM

Peaceful quiet,
Then suddenly,
Sound of planes going overhead.
Suddenly feeling scared,
Wishing you were somewhere else.
Hearing the roar
Of waves,
Crashing against the shore.
Seeing giant battleships
Out at sea.

Robert Edwards (11) Dartington CE Primary School

SEA POETRY

The big roaring sea
smashing and crashing
on the shingle
claiming millions of lives
sucking them in and spitting
them out
sometimes not spitting them out
just swallowing them whole
only to regurgitate them
in a few
years.

Edward Coveyduck (11) Dartington CE Primary School

MYSTERIOUS SLAPTON SEA

Rough wind
The wind crazily blowing the sea
rolls towards the top. Blowing and blowing it's
calling and calling the dead bodies of the sea.
Calm wind
The calm wind secretly blowing and making
the sea ripple. The breeze blowing
gently through your hair.
Sound
All the sounds, the rippling calm sea
and the crashing wild sea. The wind
whistling calling to you. The pebbles clocking
together as they get pulled back by the sea.
But the sea is just much stronger.
Secrets of Slapton
The mysterious secrets of Slapton nobody
in the whole world knows what all the
secrets are of Slapton beach. All the dead
bodies and the machinery deep deep under
the sea. The machinery rusting and the dead
bodies just bones. I know probably people
want to know a lot more about it so do I . . .

India Bourne (10) Dartington CE Primary School

AUTUMN

The sun casts a light through the trees,
The water runs over the rocks,
The birds chirp
And the wind blows -
Leaves fall from the trees.
I walk along in the woods,
The leaves crunch under my feet,
Mushrooms are everywhere.

Davey Johnson (10) Dartington CE Primary School

MIRKWOOD

Dark, black,
Never ending.
Rotting leaves,
Quiet, no wind, still,
Creepy, gloomy,
Mirkwood never ending.

Freddie Giles (11) Dartington CE Primary School

FEAR

A black pool of magic
Mixed with liquid darkness.
A dark endless room
Into a velvet ocean.
A golden peacock
With glitter eyes
That shines with bright,
all the night.
That turns from diamond
Splinters into
Liquid
pins.

Rebecca Oliver (10) Eden Park Junior School

A RAINY NIGHT

The moon is a pale, dismal face,
Half hidden by the white, wispy tresses of the clouds,
Far away as the liquid pins of rain pierce the pavements,
winds swirl like silky cotton, rolling upon the hills.
The thunder roars and growls,
Like a hungry, roaming bear.
The lightning cracks and splits the earth,
revealing flaming fire.
Slithering across the grass is a snake,
Whose back is like a wet road,
winding around endless land.
Minute golden nuggets of stars, play hide and seek
with the clouds.
Yet still the moon's dismal face,
glooms over the rainy night.

Hannah Lund (10) Eden Park Junior School

LIFE IN MY LOOKING-GLASS

As I gaze in the clear looking-glass the mirror's image glimpses back up at me.

I peer into it hard I see life, happiness, I feel I'm there, everybody hopes their worries have gone.

Without my looking-glass where would I be - staring out the window and what would I see? Nothing, just a dark grey sky, rain pouring down and sadness.

Michaela Gillard (11) Eden Park Junior School

THE DESERT

The desert
Glares at the lonely traveller
Searching for water
And offers
No help.

The desert
Burns on his cracked lip
And puts visions in his head
Of an oasis cool and refreshing
Then evaporates them away.

The desert's
Bony hand pulls him
Down into the sand
His life trickling through his body
To meet another world.

Andrew Chappell (11) Eden Park Junior School

ANGER

When someone hits me I get angry,
I feel like killing someone,
I feel like pushing someone into a volcano,
Instead I punch him,
I punch him so hard,
I make him cry,
Now,
I feel,
Worse.

Stuart Pointon (11) Eden Park Junior School

DESTRUCTION

Beyond my window,
Lies a world of greed,
The threat of creation dying,
In the cruel grip of technology,

Upon my window,
Lurks a spider,
Nesting in a web of power,
Devouring flies,

Within my window,
Woodlice gorge,
The rotting wood,

Inside my window my only power
Is to hurt others or to think,
of poems and food and lovely
birds.

Adam Dart (11) Eden Park Junior School

A STORMY NIGHT

The moon is a round white chocolate in the sky,
A pool of dreams bubbling nearby.

The night sky is a black endless room,
wind like anger brings so much doom.

Wispy grey clouds float along in the sky,
scattering diamond splinters as they pass by.

Ashley Drew (11) Eden Park Junior School

RATTLING IN THE NIGHT

Deep in the castle dungeon,
At the stroke of midnight appears,
The ghostly figure in bonds!

Its rusty chains do rattle,
As it goes up the gloomy stairs,
The ghostly figure in bonds!

To the battlements of old!
To echo his devilish screams,
The ghostly figure in bonds!

Children toss and turn in bed,
While dogs bark in dread, at,
The ghostly figure in bonds!

While all else become mere statues.
The rusty chains will rattle on,
The ghostly figure in bonds!

Matthew Bradley (10)   Eden Park Junior School

THE MIDNIGHT POEM

At night
the moon is like a silver ball
as the clouds drift by.
Thunder is like the
collision of pots and pans.
A flashing
of a torch like lightning
in the sky.
Stars are like needles pricking
in the dark.

Debbie Prosser (11)   Eden Park Junior School

THE SEA

Below the sea
Flat fish bury themselves
In the sea bed
While crabs scuttle along nervously
Trying to find traces of food.

Inside the sea
Colourful fish swim silently
And lose themselves
In a mountain of seaweed

Across the sea
Dangerous foamy topped waves
Attack the shore
And devour the cliffs
Like an angry shark

And above the sea
The blazing sun
Sends rays of sunlight
Onto the ocean
Lighting up a bird like a spotlight.

Amy Townsend (11)   Eden Park Junior School

THE CHEETAH

It is a blur in the dust
And the chase of the zebra.
It is a silkiness of fur,
It is golden eyes glowing in the jungle.
It is the spots covering a slim body,
It is the pain of the mother
Giving birth to her new-born cubs.
It is the cheetah.

Jacqueline Hazeldine (11)   Eden Park Junior School

SEA CREATURES

Dolphins leap out of the sea
Into the freshness of the waves
And the cool summer breeze
Seahorses dance
Between the tropical rocks
Swaying with coloured weed
Scared fish swerve
As sharks slide by
But on the beach
The sand like pearls
Falls through my hands.

Charlotte Brady (11) Eden Park Junior School

TROPICAL SUNSET

Glowing silky sand
Glistens like crystals on the ancient pyramids
As the sapphire sun rises
Over the ocean.

Deep in a watery grave
Tropical fish
Dart in and out of the coral
Nearby the glittering treasure winks
From a rotting shipwreck.

A golden lion prowls with the wind
Blowing its spectacular mane
Then pounces upon a ginger antelope
As the dust settles
All is still.

Jared Leaman (11) Eden Park Junior School

THE PLAYGROUND

The lonely,
Depressed playground,
Lies motionless,
Between the trees and buildings
Then suddenly,
It fills with children,
Bullies who pick on,
The scared ones,
Who hide in their own dark corners,
Or people who crowd around,
the conker matches,
Crack,
A white lace hangs loose,
There is a cry,
From the other end of the playground,
A child,
Falls hugging her knees,
The whistle blows,
And all is quiet and still,
They line up in 12 straight rows,
All is quiet,
All is dead,
And all that remains,
Of that memory,
Is a few splinters of conkers.

Christopher Moores (11) Eden Park Junior School

THE SEA

Beneath
the midnight blue sea
fish munch
through the tiny crabs.

Under the deep blue water
volcanoes erupt
sticky toxic oil
rises through the water
fish swim
through it
swallowing
and gulping
it down
soon they start
wasting away.

Throughout
the sea
storms
rain down in
rage
fish look up with
tiny staring eyes
and see
the dark sky.

Jason Redman (11) Eden Park Junior School

MUD PACK

The mud is thick
it oozes and squelches
down my magnificent horns.
I roll and splash
in the inviting slippy slime.
My fat nose
is crispy and flaky.
Even my lashes
are clogged up with it
like mascara I think.
Us girls will do
anything
for beauty.

Rhys Andrews (11) Eden Park Junior School

A POOL OF MAGIC

A pool of magic, with the moon nearby,
Glistening stars adorn the sombre sky.
A fragment of rain falls down,
from an endless sky, polishing the town.
As the rain spits at the window,
With a metallic crescendo,
A rumble of thunder grumbles in the sky.
As the wind unleashes,
Its ferocious anger grips the trees.
As the rain comes pouring down,
It sharply hits the trees and ground.
Soon appears a ribbon of moonlight,
Reflecting down, lighting up the night.

Adam True (11) Eden Park Junior School

NIGHT SKY

I adore gazing
At the dark sky.
Tonight the moon's
Encrusted core
Coats a fuzzy
Sphere of light
And hangs
On the night's sleek
Cloak. The rain's tears
Are minute silvery
Crystal pears.
Grey wisps of grit
Are clouds, stars are
Microscopic fireflies.
Thunder is a train
Blundering through the
Town while blue white
Veins of lightning
Course down through
The blackness. What
A wonder is my
Night sky.

Philip Callaghan (11) Eden Park Junior School

SPARKLING COLOURS

Where does gold live?
It lives in the traffic light
ready to go.
Is sapphire a dark colour?
Only when it's a rain cloud
floating in the sky.
What is burgundy?
The darkest night there has
ever been.
What does the colour black
see?
Deep roots twisting into the
dark soil.
What is khaki?
A magnificent rose blooming
in the summer sunset.
How old is cerise?
Older than the darkest
sparkling blue.
What two colours make
emerald? Blue and green
they live in a tropical
island.

Samantha Dorling (10) Eden Park Junior School

POTTY POEM

One white web waving
Two tiny tears teaching
Three thankless thugs thumping
Four frightful foals flicking
Five fierce fighters fishing
Six sissy sins sizzling
Seven slippery seals smoking
Eight average aircraft approaching
Nine nickname nights nipping
Ten tabby teeth talking.

Tara Willis (11) Eden Park Junior School

MEMORIES

Inside my memories lurks
Anger.
That waits to pounce on the
Helpless.
It creeps up on me and brutally
Stabs my soul.
Surrounding my memories are the
unborn dreams of life.
Throughout my memories hides
Happiness and comfort
Which drift in gentle thoughts
Of summer.
Without my memories I am
Alone and abandoned like
The playground deserted at
Night.
My memories crawl into an
Enclosed room of loneliness
Departing with my mind forever.

Hannah Foot (11) Eden Park Junior School

WHEN IT RAINS

When it rains
The grown ups say
Put up your hood
and hurry up.
They don't seem to have time to
stop so I can
Put out my tongue and try
To catch
The raindrops
on it.

When it rains
In front of us appears lots of
lovely puddles
And
The grown ups
Don't seem to have time to
Wait for me to
Go through
The muddiest
Puddle.

When it rains
Grown ups
Don't seem to be interested about
How muddy your wellies get
Or how much noise they make but
I do.
I like to hear the mud go
Squelch!
When I stand
In it.

Alice Bryant (9) Denbury CP School

MY PAINTBOX

Take
The glow of the shimmering shining
sea.
The sparkle of the rich radiant
rain.
The bluebells swaying in the wind
or the sparkle from the spring sky.
         That's blue.

Gary Addison (8) Furzeham CP School

BUBBLES

Round soft big and small shiny soggy
Very delicate I like bubbles all the
time.

Martyn Green (9) Furzeham CP School

FIREWORKS

Look look there goes one.
Bang, there's another.
A whizzing sound goes in the
sky.
Pretty colours all arrive.

Carly George (9) Furzeham CP School

THE SHIPWRECK

Seeing the terrifying sea god sent
a shivering shock down my back.
Hearing the rough crashing waves terrified
me. Feeling the water splashing on my
head. Tasting the sea water made me
sick. Smelling the fish made me very ill. Thinking
never again to see my family.

Sheldon Stokes (9) Furzeham CP School

CHRISTMAS POEM

Santa is flying in the air,
Knocking trees down there.

Rudolph's nose is bright.
All the houses in sight.

Santa delivers a gift
On his thirty-hour shift.

Santa drinks the sherry
There's a cake with a berry.

Thomas Kowalski (9) Furzeham CP School

OVER THE HILLS AND FAR AWAY

Over the hills and far away
Lived a man whose hair was grey.
He wasn't old he wasn't young.
But tired from all the work he'd done.

His face was brown and full of wrinkles.
His eyes were dark and small like winkles.
His walk was slow his back was bent.
But he really was a kindly gent.

When he smiled his face lit up.
He'd lift his hat and wish you luck.
He'd tell you tales of times gone by
And leave you with a wink of his eye.

Emma Forster (9) Furzeham CP School

SPRING

Spring is a time for new life
Fluffy new lambs bouncing in the lush new meadow.
Birds singing a lovely light tune
Robins in nests with their babies belong
Thank you for spring.

Fiona Slater (8) Furzeham CP School

SHIPWRECK

Seeing the fearsome Poseidon made me want
to scream.

Hearing the loud thunderbolt
clashing together like cymbals gave me a
headache.

Feeling the crashing waves smashing
against my chest stung.

Tasting live fish swimming into my
mouth in alarm was horrible.

The thought that I would never come
home was quite frightening.

Smelling the disgusting sea salt
made my mouth go dry.

Natasha Farmer (9) Furzeham CP School

SHIPWRECK

Seeing the terrifying sea god rise up made a
pain strike right down my spine.
Hearing the fierce roaring thunder made me feel
like I was a stiff hard stone.
Feeling the enormous freezing wave crash down
on my head felt like I was something in the freezer
at home.
Tasting the disgusting salt in the water, where
the frightening shipwreck had happened.
Smelling the horrible fishy smell that was miles
around.
Thinking I would never see my beloved parents
again made me very upset at the thought of it.

Sophie Howard (7) Furzeham CP School

MY PAINTBOX

Take . . .
The lush green from the meadow,
Take the crunch from the succulent
apples,
Take the pod from the popping green
peas,
Take the stem from the dancing
daffodils,
      That's green.

Adelaide Follon (9) Furzeham CP School

LOWRY POEM

Lowry was a famous artist.
He painted matchstick men, cats and dogs.
He was famous for his factory scenes.
He painted poor families and dull skies.
Dark colours and winter clothes
He painted matchstick figures
They all wear shabby clothes
Clogs or boots upon their feet.

Thomas Stokes (8) Furzeham CP School

SPRING POEM

Spring is lovely a new life is blossoming.
Baby lambs are being born they hop in the
warm golden sun.
There is fresh grass in the garden. Busy bees
are flying gently in the spring wind. Fiery
red roses are blossoming.
Snowdrops are sprouting through the lush green
grass.

Heidi Jones (9) Furzeham CP School

THE KITTEN

She looked outside watching the
Strange white flakes falling down on
The ground without a sound.

She jumped down from the sofa,
I opened the door,
She put out two white paws then her other pair.

Eventually her whole black body was out,
In the deep white snow.

Every step she took she jumped,
Then she ran back in,
By the warm golden brown fire.

Claire Porter (9) Furzeham CP School

THE GHOST SHIP

The ghost ship waves against the
rocks with its sharp and rusty edges.
Late at night ghosts come out to haunt
and scare the lives out of people and
sailors on boats. They soar high and low
and round in circles and they have a
frightening, haunted scary call. In the
day they disappear into dust and thin air.

Jonathan Watt (10) Furzeham CP School

THE CHEETAH

A cheetah in a desert is about
to catch its prey. Running up to
the animal jumping wildly. The cheetah
catches his meal and cuts deeply into
the animal's neck, growling fiercely with excitement,
sharpening his claws on the roots of a
tree. His glowing eyes looking for shelter
to sleep for the rest of the deadly
night and will hope to meet his prey
again tomorrow.

Luke Mills (11) Furzeham CP School

BES!

Bes is the god of children, Bes loves
dancing and music.
He loves and cares for all babies and children
with eyes as black as the night.
Bes is kind and helpful, he is as happy
as could be, and wears a head-dress of
feathers.
Bes is the protector against evil, and warns
off the evil eye.
He was found on a headrest of beds and
mirrors.

Leanne Giffard (11) Furzeham CP School

THE BLACK KITTEN

The black kitten,
As black as night,
Stood in the snow,
Miaowing with fright.

He started to walk,
With the snow chilling his tiny paws,
He stood there and stretched,
His sharp little claws.

He stood near the door,
Miaowing to get in,
There was no answer,
So he climbed in the bin.

Hayley Hemmings (10) Furzeham CP School

THE THREE LITTLE PIGS

The three chubby pigs
Went into town
And purchased some hats
And three fancy gowns.

'Oh no! Oh no! The bad wolf's come!'
And our first little weed,
Starts sucking his thumb.

'Don't be so stupid'
The second fatto cried,
But he too was ready to die.

But the third smelly pig said
'Come on guys,
Stop sitting here and,
Run for your lives!'

Hannah Martin (8) Furzeham CP School

THE GHOST

The spooky ghost,
Had a terrifying host
Its human horrid head
Was chicken stew,
so you'd better beware!
If not it might be you!
The horrific ghost
was hairy and warty (in other
words ugly!) He lived in a gloomy
and dark house, where it is
       haunted.

Rachel Shears (8) Furzeham CP School

GREEN...

Take...
Long wavy
grass, the delicate
stem of a
plant, a bouncy,
grasshopper, a
green fiery dragon
That is
green.

Mark Lovell (8) Furzeham CP School

RED

Take... beautiful rosy full lips
the shining red cars in the
sun. Crackling hot fire
and the robin's round
breast
That is red.

Stephanie Blower (9) Furzeham CP School

TAKE...

Take...
a look at the
feathery robin's
breast
smell the beautiful
roses
listen to the crackly fire.
That is red.

Victoria Milner (8) Furzeham CP School

CLOSED FOR WINTER

In the nights of the cold winter
I walk down the darkened streets
Looking into windows where bright lights once shone
The shops are closed with their big black doors.
I will never get my shopping done.
Shut, Shut, Shut that's all they do
As I pass all the people shut their doors
And in the shops the signs say 'Closed'
'Closed for winter'.

Emily Thorp (9) Furzeham CP School

SHIPWRECK

Seeing the flashing lightning gave
me the exciting feeling that I'd
never get to the safety of home.

Hearing the stormy crashing waves
gave me a shiver down the spine.

Feeling the rough black sea and
the old crabs below my feet.

Tasting the salty water the big
amounts of gooey seaweed nearly
put me fast asleep.

Smelling the oily sticky rocks
made me feel lucky to be alive.

Thinking about my beloved family
made me shout out and cry
salty tears down my cheeks.

Maria Lovell (9) Furzeham CP School

FIREWORKS

Up you go in the sky
you go bang then you die
up you go you little spark
in the dark dark dark
Bang bang bang
you're very very nice
you're just my dice.

Christopher Brizio (9) Furzeham CP School

THE SHADOWS OF THE NIGHT

I saw a horse upon the hillside
staring at me, I stared back
with fright in the night.

Its white silky coat shone bright
in the night, as it moved through
the dark shadows of the trees.

In the starlight I saw its horn
twinkling bright upon its head.
With my own eyes, I knew
it was a Unicorn.

Charlotte Hamling (9) Furzeham CP School

SPACEWAR

Stars and comets whizzing into darkness.
Pluming spaceships falling into nowhere.
A sea of stars floating and glinting.
Crunching asteroids colliding into each other.
Exploding guns firing on into the night.
War destroying everything.
Aliens rushing after humans in never-ending fight.
Roaring engines speeding on into the night.

Phillip Preston (9) Furzeham CP School

BUBBLES

B ouncy bulgy bubble floating everywhere.
U nder desks and over there.
B ouncy hypnotic planets there in outer space.
B eautiful delicate bubbles bouncing in your face.
L ittle tiny bubbles go pop and bang.
E verlasting never.
S ilently sinking through the floor.

Faye Vandenberg (10) Furzeham CP School

WATERFALL

Cool clear running water,
As clear as glass,
Hurtling down towards the ground,
Children playing noisily,
Palm trees swaying in the light jungle breeze,
White spray is flying into the air,
High above in the hilltops,
The waterfall starts as a river
t
 r
  i
   c
    k
     l
      i
       n
        g
       d
      o
     w
    n

Amy Stanford (10) Furzeham CP School

THE CHEEKY MONKEY

Skinny, hairy,
swinging along in
the trees.

That cheeky monkey.

Adam Anderson (8) Furzeham CP School

SNOW

As white as a cloud floating high in
the sky,
Cold fluffy snow as cold as ice,
Falling silently from the heavens above,
It's settled - get out,
Crisp crunch breaking it for the first
time,
Isn't snow wonderful.

Mark Smith (11) Furzeham CP School

THE BUBBLES

The bubbles come out of the
ring like a wobbly jelly. They float
like a bird gliding in the sky.
Land like rain and pop like a
balloon. They drift very slowly
but pop very fast. They are very
colourful and delicate and fragile.
They touch the ground very gently and
bounce like a ball when they land
they pop and some land but do
not last more than five seconds.

Andrew Binmore (10) Furzeham CP School

AUTUMN

Leaves falling gently from the trees
Covering the path I walk alone.
Conkers cracking on the ground
Making a wonderful crunchy sound.
A squirrel scampers up a tree
To hide his nuts for the winter.

Jonathan Tozer (9) Furzeham CP School

SPRING

Spring spring wonderful spring.
Spring is the time of year
when dancing darting daffodils sprout
out from their cosy winter's nap.
Blossom blooming brightly with
colours like piercing yellow, fiery red and
pearl blue. Birds singing softly as
they glide swiftly through the tall
twisting trees.

Christopher Cornish (9) Furzeham CP School

SPRING IS THE TIME

Spring is the time for apple trees
With grass popping up in a nice warm sun
With blossoms and daffodils staring at you
With your dad cutting your garden's grass
Birds flying past you in a wonderful blue sky.

Michael Williams (8) Furzeham CP School

WAR POEM

The gruesome sight that I see
The damage and destroyed houses of my neighbours.
The bombing and sudden banging and sirens going off
and gasmasks going on.
I feel sad, gloomy and frightened.
I thought of the brave heroic people
Who have the courage to die, just to help us
live in England. How could Germany do this to us?
It's spoiled our country.
I hope a bomb doesn't land right next to me
I might be killed.

Nicola Parton (9) Furzeham CP School

CLASS 5 POEM

There's a boy in my class who keeps on talking
There's a girl in my class who keeps on laughing
There's a grumpy teacher who keeps on telling me off
then he says 'Sin bin at one o'clock'.
Jack thinks he is a cool dude and Adelaide thinks she's
a Pringle
and Nicola thinks she's a bottle of Coke and Laura
thinks she's a Highlander.
When we make models out of clay they always
seem to break at the end of the day.

Christopher Williams (8) Furzeham CP School

SPRING

Spring has blossomed all around
Fluffy clouds dancing in the sky.
Daffodils popping out of the ground.
Sparkling sun on the lush green grass.
Red fiery roses burst into flower.

It's spring.

Harriet Mealey (8) Furzeham CP School

SPRING

Spring is a time for change where lambs
are bouncing beautifully in the meadow.
The sky is bright and beautiful.
Birds singing sweetly in the blossoming trees.
Spring blossomed again.

Michelle Binmore (8) Furzeham CP School

CLASS 5

Add, take, times and share
Fit together like a pair.
Telling the time is easy
ABC is peasy. 123 is cool
And we act the fool.
PE is number one and the story has
just begun.

Ben Strike (8) Furzeham CP School

THE SEASIDE

I love the seaside
The waves splash
on me.
I love the seaside
I paddle in the sea.
I love the seaside
The sun shining on me.
I love the seaside
and it loves me.

Louise Thorp (10) Gatehouse Primary School

DREAMLAND

In my dreamland I do see
A crystal clear sparkling sea
All joy and happiness
Never fear
No-one there ever sheds a tear.

Mum storms in and says 'Come
on sleepy head
Time to get up and out of bed.'
'No' I reply 'just hold my
hand.
I want to go back to
my dreamland.'

Jessica Pickup (10) Gatehouse Primary School

THE SEASIDE

The crashing
waves upon the
sand.
And the pounding
of the drum
in the band.
I sit there staring
at the seaside
watching the
crashing and
banging tide.

Emma Caple (10) Gatehouse Primary School

UNDER THE SEA

Whales and dolphins swimming
to and fro.
Mermaids playing with ball to
throw.
Small fish, big fish
fat and thin fish.
Some are silver
some are gold.
A baby whale I was to
hold.
Crabs with colours blue, pink
and grey.
A mermaid came and
asked me to play.

Joanna Lever (11) Gatehouse Primary School

MONSTERS!

Monsters in the night
Monsters in the night
They hide in the cupboard
And they give you a big fright at night!
Ah!

Rachel Clark (10) Gatehouse Primary School

UNTITLED

It's fast and furious
F1 racing,
people cheer to go
into gear,
The cars change every year,
faster and faster till . . .
Crash!

Tom Bellamy (10) Gatehouse Primary School

MUD

Mud is slimy sticky
gooey runny messy
repulsive. Filled with
worms slugs and insects.
Who could like the horrid stuff?
If you fall and slip into it
You make an awful mess.

Helen O'Brien (9) Gatehouse Primary School

UNDER THE SEA!

Seaweed blowing with the current
Corals and a chest of pearls
Rocks and bubbles in clear water
Soft sand, sea-horses and a ray
Scuttle crab, dolphins and a whale
Little stones that look like hail
This is what I saw today.

Emily McLaughlan (11) Gatehouse Primary School

UNDER THE SEA

Beneath the great sea
Stripy fish swim around me
Crabs and sting rays from above
Sand and rocks are really rough.

Ben Chambers (11) Gatehouse Primary School

KELLY!

There was a girl called Kelly,
Who kept on watching the telly.
She said 'Oh my,
I've got a square eye,
And my legs feel just like jelly.'

Kelly Lomas (11) Gatehouse Primary School

MY DARKEST DAY

When somebody is ill
We are worried.
When somebody dies
We are sad.
We cry in dismay,
We are devastated
And angry and mad
Will we ever be happy again?

We will always remember them
We still have our memories
We can look at the photographs
The pain is easing now
Perhaps we can be happy again.

Michael Ayling (11) Gatehouse Primary School

UNDER THE SEA

Blue sea
golden sand
you can't hear anything
I can see just one little
fish swimming around
and around.
Just a tiny dot in the big
blue sea.
It is really good because
I'm under the sea.

Richard Williams (10) Gatehouse Primary School

UNDER THE SEA

The warm blue sea
had pink and orange coral,
some crabs with short legs,
an eel with seaweed stuck to it,
it feels like a dream,
rocks with fish coming in and out.
Am I awake?
Or am I asleep?
A fish swims past
a big striped fish,
I see the sparkling sun,
it is yellow and big,
I wish I was one.

Amy Martin (10) Gatehouse Primary School

GROWING UP OR NOT!

I'm growing up.
I'm looking forward
to things that are to come.
I think I might
try to grow up fast
or stay in the past
where I belong.

Gemma Crawford (11) Gatehouse Primary School

DAWLISH

The sea is calm as the water
from your tap only it's thicker
water than sea water. The people
are nice and friendly. When the people
walk by the river in Dawlish they always
feed the black swans in the Bibrook.
The trees are bare in the autumn
down by the Bibrook.

Leighton Frost (9) Gatehouse Primary School

THE TOURISTS

The tourists swim around Dawlish
like ants in an anthill,
The swans swim as gracefully
as a stream. The red rock is
as hollow as a beehive.
People laugh like a hyena.
I like Dawlish I like my home.

Matthew Hogg (9) Gatehouse Primary School

DAWLISH HAS?

Dawlish has black swans as
black as ink. Bamboo as strong as
steel or rock. Dawlish beach as
gold as the Queen's crown. Summer
is as hot as two suns stuck
together. The sea like millions of
sapphires, pearls and emeralds
sparkling and glinting in the sun.
Dawlish is surrounded by things no
one or no thing would ever think of.
I like Dawlish don't you?

Adam Willis (9) Gatehouse Primary School

DAWLISH

The tourist walks around all
day like a busy bee,

That's Dawlish for you.

The sea shouts out like
a god, calling all the people in,

That's Dawlish for you.

The black swan is as black
as night and swims as
swift as a fish,

That's Dawlish for you.

Annie Connell (9) Gatehouse Primary School

DAWLISH SWANS

Dawlish moves like bees
As fast as a cheetah
The swans swim as the stream goes.
The swans are as dark as night
and as light as day
When it rains it's like a flood
and there's a lot of green
and a lot of blue.

Matthew Hodgson (9) Gatehouse Primary School

POEM OF DAWLISH

The town is as busy as bees,
Roaming like the wind,
You can't get away from the lawn,
It's always packed with things from the breeze.

It's like a beehive,
All active at day,
But when the night comes,
It's all gone away.

Louise Hogg (9) Gatehouse Primary School

DAWLISH

The tourists are as busy as bees,
Roaming about the town,
When the tourists go back to their hives,
It's round about night time!

The sea is as rough as a boxer,
But people still go swimming!
When they go back to their hives
It is also still night-time!

Ellen Williams (9) Gatehouse Primary School

THE SEA AND SAND

People swim in the sea
and use rubber rings.
Blow-up boats and other
things. Fishing round
the rock pools.
Catching fish all day
and building sand
castles. In the summer
it's as busy as a fish
getting chased by
a shark.

Anthony Banning (9) Gatehouse Primary School

LONELINESS

Loneliness
    I hate the word
Like jam and mustard
    and lemon curd.
Peanut butter and
    chocolate spread
I eat before
    I go to bed
My parents disapprove
    of that
So I cry and cry and
    hug the cat.
That fateful day I
    went to school
I thumped and kicked
    and broke the rule
So I got sent to the
    head teacher's office
and had a meeting with
    Mr McRoffice
Finally I made
    some friends
and they asked me to join
    their gang 'the nerds'.

Jenna Bettinson (11) Gatehouse Primary School

HOLLY

There once was a girl called Holly
Who was a bit of a wally.
She was really sad
So she called to her dad
'Oh gosh I've lost my dolly.'

Ricky North (11) Gatehouse Primary School

UNDER THE SEA

Calm is the sea where starfish live,
They drift when anything moves.
I wish they had faces so then they could see
The striped fish swimming along.

Purple green and blue
They're the colours I knew.
They hide behind rocks
Why aren't they me?

Starfish I see in a clear blue sea,
Seaweed drifting around,
Fish with their babies:
Big ones
Small ones.
Wish they could hear me
Wish they could hear.

Kerry Shields (10) Gatehouse Primary School

UNDER THE SEA

I step, my feet are warm in the white sand,
Blue, red and yellow fish swim around me,
A shark hunting in deeper water,
I see the coral, spiny and sharp,
I touch it, my finger bleeds,
the salt water washes the blood away.
The stingrays swimming around me,
brown and speckled and some white,
they swim slowly, but elegantly
their tails streaming behind them.
The sun makes them look so graceful.

Matthew Heaton (11) Gatehouse Primary School

UNDER THE SEA

Under the sea it's quiet and clear,
The sand was light grey and nothing I
could hear.
It was the greatest feeling
Like I was free.
It's so great to be under the sea.
Multi-coloured fish on the pale grey sand.
They swam straight past my hand.

Joanne Osborne (11) Gatehouse Primary School

JOANNA

Joanna is a CD player on loud,
A beefburger with chips
She's a calm drizzle with
sudden thunder,
Joanna is a small sports
car but fast,
Fizzy cola that suddenly
goes flat,
Absolutely Fabulous in the
boring bits,
Purple, crimson with rage,
A cheater, she can't change
her spots.

Leigh Toney (11) Gatehouse Primary School

UNDER THE SEA

When I'm under the sea
I see
Fish with black and white spots
Even some with dots
And green seaweed waving on the rocks

When I'm under the sea
I see
Fish with blue and red stripes
All different types
And green seaweed waving on the rocks

When I'm under the sea
I see
Jellyfish swimming around
Not knowing I was around
And green seaweed waving on the rocks.

Sarah Brimacombe (11) Gatehouse Primary School

UNDER THE SEA

      Lapping waves
      Magic crabs
Silky warm water
All under the sea.
Why is it like this?
      Don't ask me!
      Clear gold sand
        Not a rock in sight
I am warm
I am staying here all night.

Laura Jewell (10) Gatehouse Primary School

UNCOMFORTABLE MAN!

David is big uncomfortable
furniture
Not a good meal
Sometimes bad weather
He's a small vehicle
and a bad drink
He's X-files
a big red person
and a bit of a hard man.

Michelle Carter (11) Gatehouse Primary School

THE FROG

I was a dot
surrounded by jelly
not much fun
quite boring really,

I don't know my father
or mother at all
all of my family
live next door,

I was soon to be growing
breaking free
a new life ahead
would be good for me,

After I'd grown a bit
and got a tail
I swam far away
to a space of my own,

Now I have freedom
my space to grow
soon I'll have legs
then lose my tail,

I've done these things now
I'm a fully grown frog
just think what I started as
a small little dot.

Daisy Lang (10) High Bray CP School

STORM

The storm blows, the gale screams,
with the big trees rustling,
And the big whining wind,
with the big screams whistling,
The blows and the puffs, the howls and screams,
with the big yawns whispering,
The crashes and the screeches,
The thunder and the lightning,
and big moans with the big whines,
and the big blustery crashing and creaking.

Gessica Boddington (9) High Bray CP School

STORM

The rain thumping against the windows,
The wind screeching and lightning crashing,
With the stormy hurricane across the land,
And whirlwind whistles with a whine

The blustery gust that whips the windows,
And the thunder stings with a creak,
And the wind rustles with a sigh.

Hurricanes blowing with puffs of screams,
Tornado destroys the houses with a moan
The gales shrieking and people screaming
The rain and hail devastates houses.

Amanda Childs (9) High Bray CP School

WHAT'S THIS ANIMAL?

I was in my egg,
All tucked up inside
When all of a sudden,
I started to cry.

My egg was cracking,
It was so cold,
This reason why,
I was so bold.

I hopped from my egg,
All quivered and cold,
My new life ahead of me,
I was to be sold.

I'm growing hair
All fluffy and cuddly.
I'm trying to fly
But it's all too muddly.

After some months
I'm growing old
I'm laying eggs
All to be sold.

I'm growing too old
All shaky and dying
I wonder what's next
Oh I feel like crying.

The farmer shot me
I've lived a long life
I'm on a plate
Being carved by a knife.

Hannah Robins (10) High Bray CP School

STORM

Sitting in the sitting room,
Listening to the hail,
While I sit there and think,
I can hear the wind wail.

The whirlwind whispers and wails,
The wind goes quiet,
The hail now does trail,
It all goes quiet.

Emma Crawford (9) High Bray CP School

THE STORM

The wind is howling the storm is growling
Babies crying people dying.
The waves are crashing lightning is flashing.
Cars are crashing, people screaming, trees leaning.

Andrew Pink (10) High Bray CP School

THE STORM

A stormy night all bright was crashing down
Wind blowing wind hailing all night breaking things
Rain crashing, wind singing
Waves crashing the wind howls and screams
The storm is starting the wind wails
A gust of wind can blow things over and make houses fly away.
I am in the sitting room listening outside for a flight.

Chloe Jemmison (8) High Bray CP School

BUTTERFLIES

I came out of my cocoon
I smelt the air
I flapped my wings
And I flew off
After a while

I flew for food
I ate some nectar
I fell asleep.

Kelly Lane (9) High Bray CP School

MY HOUSE POEM

Once I was standing
But now I'm just crumbled
Oh I'm so sad.

Oh I wish I was as new as new
But I doubt that wish will come true
Oh I'm so sad.

Joe Doyle (9) High Bray CP School

STORM

The storm is coming and wind is smashing,
There is something bad in the air.

The storm is pinching the storm is stinging,
There is something bad in the air.

The leaves all rustle the rain is slashing,
There is something bad in the air.

The lightning crashes with silver lashes,
There is something bad in the air.

The storm arrives with rage and anger,
There is something bad in the air.

Thunder bangs, puffs and wind howls,
There is something bad in the air.

Rain clouds empty themselves,
There is something bad in the air.

Hailstones drop from the dark grey sky,
There is something bad in the air.

Homes destroyed by the furious gale,
The wind whistles the wind sings,
There is something bad in the air.
There is something bad in the air.

Bridie Stevens (10) High Bray CP School

PIRANHA

Bone strippers
That's what we are
Fall in the swamp
Dead meat
That's you dead.
Sharp teeth
Fins small but lethal
We'll strip your bones.
Bone strippers
That's what we are
In ten minutes, your bones.
It's a Christmas treat
If we meet
To me not to you
Run! Too late
Sharp teeth bite
I'm sorry
So what! Nice meal.
Bone strippers
That's what we are.

Sam Way (8) Newton St Cyres Primary School

I'D LIKE TO BE A TADPOLE

I'd like to be a tadpole,
And live in a swampy pond
I'd never have to change my clothes,
Or wash my dirty socks.

I'd like to be a tadpole,
And live in a weedy pond
I'd never have to wash the dishes,
Or get told off by my mum.

I'd like to be a tadpole,
And live in a really clean pond
I'd never have to do my maths,
Or learn all of my spellings.

But then . . .

I'd hate to be a tadpole,
And live in a dirty pond
I might get eaten,
Or caught by a human.

Emma Hodge (9) Newton St Cyres Primary School

DEEP IN THE CELLAR

Deep in the cellar
What do you hear?
People dying
Bats squealing.

Deep in the cellar
Water falling
What do you feel?
Scared
Water trickling down your head

Deep in the cellar
What is hiding?
Spiders, rats, bats
Lurking in the shadows.

Holly Delve (8) Newton St Cyres Primary School

THIS IS THE FOOT

This is the foot
that stepped in some jelly
that went on my foot
and it was very cold.

This is the foot
that fell in a puddle
that got very wet
and very slippery.

This is the foot
that went in my shoe
that took me for a walk
in the sunshine.

This is the foot
that went in my shoe
that fell in a puddle.

This is the foot
that never gets lost.

Sarah Stephen (9) Newton Poppleford School

AUTUMN TIME

Sitting on the highest branch of the highest tree,
Looking out for shiny conkers to see,
Looking out for squirrels climbing up a nearby tree,
Looking out for falling leaves,
Looking out for squirrels collecting nuts for
                         autumn hibernation,
Looking out for acorns falling on the crispy floor,
Listening out for an acorn to fall in the cold stream.

Michael McDonald (8) Newton Poppleford School

LIMERICK

There was a young girl called Jo,
Who found a big red bow,
She put it on her dress,
And said 'That's the best,'
And to a great grand ball she did go.

Jodie Peters (9) Newton Poppleford School

PUSSY PUSSY PUDDLE CAT

Pussy, pussy, puddle cat,
What do you think you're playing at
Making puddles on the mat?
Don't do that!

Victoria Sykes (8) Newton Poppleford School

A LIMERICK

There once was a girl called Jess,
Who had a long fancy dress,
She went to a ball,
And slipped up in the hall,
And ended up in a terrible mess.

Jessica Tubbs (8) Newton Poppleford School

THANK YOU

It's easy to say 'Thank you,'
It shows how much we care,
We should say it more often,
Then it wouldn't be quite so rare.
It makes other people happy,
Especially our parents, teachers and friends,
So remember to say 'Thank you,'
Then someone will some day thank you!

Seline Rodgers (9) Newton Poppleford School

A SAPPHIRE CAT

A sapphire cat,
On the door mat,
How did it get there?
It didn't move a hair!
It was all blue,
Then up to my room I flew,
When I came back it had gone
           in a puff of smoke!

Megan Rodgers (9) Newton Poppleford School

THE TALLEST TREE

As I sit under the tallest tree,
Watching leaves scrunch under feet,
Watching the farmer cutting the wheat,
Watching the leaves all golden brown,
Watching the lights go on in the town,
Watching the birds fly away with their new-born,
Watching the farmer cutting the corn,
Watching the leaves fall to the ground,
Watching the children playing around,
Watching the hunter shooting things down,
Watching the boy that looks like a clown,
I like it here it's nice and peaceful.

Mark Broughton (9) Newton Poppleford School

STORM

    Pitter patter
        cold
            wet
                showers,
splashing
rivers
            storms,
gushing
      raindrops
         drip.

from
  the
    sky.

Darren Bennett (8) Newton Poppleford School

A SPELL FOR MACBETH

Hubble bubble boil and trouble . . .

The bad tooth of a dog
A dog's bad tooth

The slimy tongue of a toad
A toad's slimy tongue

The rotting wing of a bat
A bat's rotting wing

The pecking beak of an owl
An owl's pecking beak

The hairy tail of a wolf
A wolf's hairy tail

Hubble bubble boil and trouble . . .

Belinda Rowse (8) Newton Poppleford School

DRAGONS

Dragons
Ruin homes
And I do not like them so . . .
Go away dragons!
Oh go away dragons!
No, do not stay.

Oliver Jones (9) Newton Poppleford School

WAVES CRASHING

I look at the sea,
I see waves crashing on rocks,
Rolling and tumbling.

Carly Olliff (8) Newton Poppleford School

PEOPLE

On a hot sunny day children at play
Out in the grounds fooling around.

Mums pushing prams, people on trams.
Some are happy, some are sad,
Some are good, some are bad.

Whoever they are they should always have handy,
T-shirt, hat, sun block to make them look dandy.

Remember one thing, sun isn't the answer,
If you don't want to die young of the killer

Skin cancer.

Amy Jones (9) Newton Poppleford School

RAINDROPS

Raindrops, raindrops,
you come out of
the sky, you are
so clear just
like the sky.

> Raindrops, raindrops,
> you are just
> a bit of water
> who is up in
> the sky.

Raindrops, raindrops,
you come to the
ground so fast
but you belong
up in the clouds.

> Raindrops, raindrops,
> you come from the
> sky, there are so
> many raindrops
> up in the sky.

Raindrops, raindrops,
you make a big
puddle, soon you
will drop to make
a bigger puddle.

Simon Ellery (11) Pilton Bluecoat Junior School

SPLASH

Water running down the stream
Every time I hear a scream
Waves going splish, splash, splosh,
I'm wearing a mackintosh

Sometimes I go to the stream
Then I see a gleam
                of light.
Puddles puddles everywhere
Then I stop and stare.

I see my foot in the puddle
Then I'm in trouble.
I think streams are fun
When you play in the sun.

I really enjoy a splash
I've got to dash.
      Bye!

Kimberley Large (11) Pilton Bluecoat Junior School

RAINDROP

R ain falls from the sky,
A ll the animals are getting dry.
I slands can float on water,
N ations surrounded by water.
D rops falling from the sky,
R iver flowing by.
O ceans that I can just see from the corner of my eye.
P itter patter on the floor the raindrops are soaking the wild boar.

Ryan Saunders (11) Pilton Bluecoat Junior School

SPRING SEASON

Flowers shoot along the riverside
While little blue tits try to hide.
Little chicks and kittens are born.
Little mice play inside the corn.
The sun is bright and makes you warm
While little bumble bees come buzzing in swarms.
In spring at Easter Jesus died for us all.
In spring you can hear the sheep run and call.
The waterfalls catch the sun's reflection.
When Easter comes you hear chocolate mentioned.
Winter has left us there's no more snow.
In spring you play as time goes slow.

Lora Gail Jones (10) Pilton Bluecoat Junior School

RAINDROPS

R ain comes down very often
A raindrop splashed on the roof top
I hope it stops soon because I want to
   go out to play
N o no, the rain will not go away soon
D rat it rain just go away!
R ain rain go away come back another
   day
O yes the rain stops
P please mum can I go out? Please!
S un is out let us go out please. Yes
   you can go out.

Kevin Jordan : Pilton Bluecoat Junior School

WINTER IS AN OLD MAN

Winter
is an old man
puffing out
wind.

His dark
blue eyes,
are the sky
ready to snow

Winter's an old man
his beard is the
clouds.

        Winter is an old man,
        his breath is
        frost and ice

                When the
                spring comes
                he dies

                Like the winter dies
                into spring.

Sam Lane (10) Pilton Bluecoat Junior School

RIVERS

Rivers rivers everywhere
Flowing like the toss of hair,

Silent rivers hidden away
Sun shining down what a beautiful day,

Tumbling rivers waterfall
From the bottom it's terribly tall,

It starts in the hills comes out in the sea
I go for a dip comes up to my knee,

Rivers are beautiful all over the place
Look into one you can see your face,

All of these rivers are different in ways
Some are near mountains some are near bays.

Helen Rendle (11) Pilton Bluecoat Junior School

WEATHER

Weather changing all the year round
Sometimes up sometimes down.
Always changing from rain to shine
Wet and windy, I wish it was mine.
How I could change it whenever I wanted
But being haunted by darkened souls.
All alone, and spirits begin to roam,
Throughout the streets,
Lost the joy they had after the summer heats.
Never again should I be clever,
And try to control the world's weather.

Tom Wade (11) Pilton Bluecoat Junior School

WATERFALLS

Waterfall, waterfall
falling down, it only
stops hits the
ground.

                    Waterfall, waterfall
                    splat on the ground
                    like a fried egg
                    swishing round and
                    round.

Waterfall, waterfall
you're so clear
swishing around
like Jason
McAteer.

                    Waterfall, waterfall
                    likes to drink he
                    doesn't have water
                    he gets beer from
                    his sink.

Waterfall, waterfall
you're so deep
until you hit the
ground and end
up in a heap.

Tom Ireland (11) Pilton Bluecoat Junior School

CHRISTMAS TIME

      Starlight is shining bright,
      Sparkling through this Christmas night.
      Ringing bells in the sky
      Is it Santa coming by?
      Santa says ho, ho, ho!
      Coming through the deep white snow.
Toys piled up on his sleigh,
I hope he's coming my way.
As he comes through the drifts,
Bringing all my lovely gifts
As I lay fast asleep,
He brings me presents to keep.

Christopher Kingdon (11) Pilton Bluecoat Junior School

SCHOOL CLOCK

S chool clock in the hall,
C lock is hanging on the wall,
H anging there watching things,
O h he hates it when teacher sings,
O h he dreams of the classroom,
L oathing the loud sighs of gloom.

C lock is usually very wrong,
L oud is his untimely gong,
O peration, operation mend the clock,
C lock will soon be going tick, tock,
K eep your time old school clock.

Clare Tanner (11) Pilton Bluecoat Junior School

WINTER TIME

It's always pouring the sun's not shining,
My little sister is always whining,
It's cold out, so I was told,
And all the trees are going bald.
Rivers are all frozen over,
My dad's washing the Rover.
My fingers are all numb,
And so is my thumb.
The blue, black and grey,
Are colours in every way.
Turkeys all get cooked,
Our holiday's already booked.
Animals will get fed,
I always read in bed.

Karen Ten-Bokkel (10) Pilton Bluecoat Junior School

TREES

Trees are old and crusty they live
for many years.
And you can hide under
them when the sky sheds tears.
There are a lot of different trees
like willow, elm and pine.
I wish there were more trees
but they will come in time.
Some have sticky leaves, some
are thin and long,
And when the wind
whistles through them they
sing a quiet song.

Lizzie Bunyan (10) Pilton Bluecoat Junior School

CATS

Some little kittens
Are the size of mittens
Some old cats
Are quite fat.

    In the morning waking up
    The cat is there watching a pup
    Waiting to be fed
    Looking like it's dead

As I open the cupboard where the food sits
Suddenly my cat's eyes lit
As he saw the food come out
And putting it in he had a doubt

    When I was gone
    The food was gone
    Then when he sleeps
    I have a little peep
    I felt like a sneak

I have a cat called Bubbles
And I sometimes get muddled.

Lauren Hole (10) Pilton Bluecoat Junior School

MY LIFE

I like my mother but not my brother.
I like my bat but not my rat.
I like Sunday but not Monday.
I like baking but not waiting.
My dad is *thirty* and my dog is dirty.
I don't like yellow but I like marshmallow.

Christopher Williams (10) Pilton Bluecoat Junior School

THE RIVER RIDE

It starts as a trickling ripple,
Eagerly joining other streams.
It ends as a swift flowing river,
With its mouth to the sea.

On its journey to its destiny,
It will dart and swerve and sway and pour,
Building up more and more,
On its course through the valley, it will twist and turn
                                          and slide,
Trying to catch up with the winding tide.

The glistening river cascades over a hill,
Making a waterfall that would give you a chill.
It will push and plunge and erode the rock,
This is not a place where you could dock.

Then when you finally get to the mouth of the river to
                                  where it joins the sea,
Also known as the estuary,
After all that darting and swerving and swaying and
pouring and twisting and turning and sliding and
blinding and winding and cascading and pushing and
                                  plunging and eroding,
It finally finishes its journey,
Which took it to the sea.

Jenny Smith (11) Pilton Bluecoat Junior School

THE SPLASHING RIVER

It starts as a trickle,
It trickles into streams,
The streams form rivers, splashing and crashing.
Rivers zoom down hills,
Getting faster and faster.
At the end of the hill,
The river slows down,
And is no longer violent until,
It goes cascading over waterfalls,
Falling through the air.
It passes rabbits, foxes and hares.
It swims with otters,
It races the horses,
It is blocked by beavers and then,
It slows down and reaches the sea,
Then it is violent once more.

Corwin Easey (10) Pilton Bluecoat Junior School

WHO?

Evil, ugly and smelly
He likes his Cola and jelly.
He stays in the kitchen all day
long, I can see his polka dots
and they look all wrong and his
ugly purple hair.
I hate it when he stares at me
because he's got an ugly looking glare.

Charlie Falco (9) Pilton Bluecoat Junior School

MY DANCING RIVER

The trees hang over,
Calm and still.
The glittering sun is peeping through,
The dancing river rushing down.
Cascading down a waterfall,
Joining other rivers eagerly.
Wearing away the waterfall,
Eating the banks to nothing.
The birds sing and dance,
Where the fish watch far away.
They open their mouths to the sea,
Other rivers come and join them.
Running to and fro,
Down to the wild sea.
Eroding as I go,
Down near the estuary.
My dancing river.

Natalie Hole (11) Pilton Bluecoat Junior School

FEAR!

Upstairs, all alone, all dark
floorboards are creaking
but everyone is sleeping.
A hairy tarantula is crawling up my bed
and on to my hair and head.
In the morning I wake up and realise
it was just the shadows on the wall.

Hannah Chapple (10) Pilton Bluecoat Junior School

LIKES AND DISLIKES POEM

Waking up with school ahead
makes me want to stay in bed
up and down the swimming pool
makes me feel a bit of a fool.
Listening to the squealing mice
makes me want to eat Chinese rice.
Boys can be a bit of a pain
and my mother drives me insane.
I don't like it when we do tests
but I like it when we have guests.
I really like eating food
but I hate it when people are rude.
I really don't like having baths
and I don't like going up and down paths.
I really like having a Hocking's ice-cream
I don't like it when people scream.

Bethany Cole (9) Pilton Bluecoat Junior School

ANTHONY BIRCHMORE

He likes doing goblin faces
but he doesn't like doing up
his laces.
He gets grumpy and sometimes
frumpy.
He's average height and
very light
even though he's very
funny
he reminds
me of a little
bunny.

Sarah Lake (10) Pilton Bluecoat Junior School

DRAGON IN THE HOUSE

Is there a dragon in the house?
Is it fat or is it thin?
What is that noise in the house?
Is it the dragon who is getting ready to burn me?
I don't know, do you know?
What is that bang on the roof?
It might be the dragon taking us away to his cave.
Oh no it is opening the door.
Help! Oh no it's only my dad but who is
                            making that noise?
As I look out the window I see a dragon going.
As I watch the dragon go I see it saying goodbye.

Jason Western (9) Pilton Bluecoat Junior School

I LIKE CHOCOLATE

I like chocolate
I get in a mess
Mum gets cross when I get it on my dress.

My favourite chocolate is Wispa
because it has holes.

I go to a party and eat
all the chocolate rolls.

I have Rice Crispy cakes
and have them for my lunch.

When I get one in my hand
I munch and munch and munch.

I like fishing with bait and eating
Choc-o-late!

Christina Bloor (10) Pilton Bluecoat Junior School

FISHING POEM

You cast your rod in and
  wait for a bite, quick, quick
    we've got a bite. You reel
      your rod in, you've
        got a fish.
          You run home
            saying
              'We've got our dinner tonight!'

Anthony Birchmore (10) Pilton Bluecoat Junior School

FRED

Fred is my friend
I like him a lot
I'll never let the stupid French
put him in the pot.
I keep him in a little box
with a margarine tub
I give him flies and bits of meat
for his grub.
He can jump very high
as high as me.
He can nearly jump as high
as a tiny little flea.
I found him in my garden
at the bottom of the hedge.
I thought of lots of names
like Johnny, Tim or Reg.
I thought and thought and thought
of names in my head
when I suddenly had the bright idea
I'll call him Fred.

Freya McCaie (10) Pilton Bluecoat Junior School

MAGICAL LAND

I'm sure I went into a magical land
Where the beaches are full of golden sand
Where animals talk
And trees listen to what I say
Until the break of day.
Sunrises blue, pink and yellow
Sunsets are orange, red and yellow
I heard nice music come from a far off land
While I was in this magical land.
There is no winter in this magical world
No autumn
Just spring and summer
With their exotic flowers.

Daniel Stancombe (10) Pilton Bluecoat Junior School

ON MY BIRTHDAY

My birthday was on Saturday 11th May.
I had a lovely party that day.
I had loads of presents and a birthday cake.
We watched a video about a panda.
People got the panda and the baby panda
                 was up in the tree
Then the two children were
trying to get the panda back.
We played Barbie dolls.

Sarah Wellington (10) Pilton Bluecoat Junior School

THE SCARY NIGHT

A ship was coming
It was going to crash into a submarine
It was going faster every minute
The submarine was near a volcano
The volcano was going to explode any minute
The ship was going to crash
It was dreadful
Everything was moving too fast
The people in the submarine
And the people in the ship were frightened
Everybody was scared and frightened
The volcano was going to erupt in 35 minutes
They were so frightened that they
                            couldn't breathe or move
Bang!
Went the volcano
The people in the ship screamed
The people in the submarine shouted 'Help! Help!'

Rebecca Graham (9) Princetown CP School

A LIMERICK

A young boy who thought he was flash
Leapt into the pool with a splash
But when he was in he fell on a pin
And screamed out 'I'll sell it for cash.'

Rebekka Devey (11) Princetown CP School

DEAD OF NIGHT

I shiver when lightning
streaks through the sky.
I am scared
and it is dark.
I hear the waves colliding
with the rocks
I am scared and
it is dark.
I hear the screech of an owl in
the night.
My ears and
face are covered
in sweat.
I was scared
and it was dark.
I ran to my
mum's room
but there
was nothing
there except
a monstrous bloodthirsty
bat!
I ran for my life.
Suddenly I
felt sharp
fangs
pierce
my skin.
I was truly dead.

Harry Forbes (9) Princetown CP School

THE VOLCANO

It was all quiet then
A volcano was about to erupt, rumble rumble.
Then crash, thunder and lightning strike
Big rocks came crashing down
It was a very cold night
Owls hooted
Wind blew
There was another sudden flash of thunder and
Lightning.
I trembled with fear
Then it went quiet
Something was behind me
I turned round
I saw nothing
I wanted to turn around and run
I felt the warmth of the volcano
I was scared
I ran with the lightning chasing me
Then suddenly it was quiet
I felt the lava coming closer
I was very frightened
I heard some rocks crash behind me
It was dark and still
The rough sea crashed up against the rocks
I was wet and shivering
It was foggy
There was a creaking noise behind me
I was miserable and scared
The sea went calmer
The thunder and lightning died away
The sea calmed down.

Emma Garrett (9) Princetown CP School

THE VOLCANO

One night a volcano erupted.
The lava came rumbling down,
Rumble, rumble, stones came down
Smack, I was scared
I looked behind me
and I saw red stuff.
I thought it was my imagination
I was scared.
Then I saw a volcano,
Lava! Lava!
Go away, oh please!
I was shivering all over
I started to run but the lava was
Right behind me.
I didn't know what to do.
I screamed for help.
No-one answered
I ran into town shouting
Help!

Adam Garrett (8) Princetown CP School

A BIT OF LOVE

Your eyes are blue
Your hair is blonde
Your face is pink
Your heart is red
Your heart is warm
And your heart is for
One girl to set it
      free.

Tammy Pidgeon (9) Princetown CP School

THE NOTHING

I ran and ran
I kept running
The lightning struck again
The sky lit up
Then it went black again
The clouds came over the moon
It got dark, very dark.
I could hear it coming
The ground rumbled
You could hear it coming
Coming to get you.
The *nothing* came!
It destroyed everything in its path
It caught up with me
It took me away
It stopped everything
I fell to the ground
It was all back to normal.
It was odd.

Adam Court (9) Princetown CP School

WAR ZONE

I see a lady getting her shopping
I hear a baby crying.
I feel my spine shivering

Now I see my mum and dad getting taken away.
Now I hear them crying my name Graham help me help me.
Now I feel nothing at all because my mum and dad have been
Taken away.

Graham Sargent (10) Princetown CP School

WAR

War is beginning
The ship is like cold and
wet wood.
Storm is coming.

      I feel frightened.

Viking ships are coming
Across the rough sea.

      Don't give up!

Suddenly war stopped
The ships went home
And the people in
Princetown were safe
Even in town it was
safe too.
      but I felt frightened.

Charlene O'Neill (9) Princetown CP School

THE TERRIBLE STORM

Thunder and lightning crashing on the sea.
A volcano is erupting tonight.
A war is beginning.
Fighting and dying in the storm.
Power lines cut down.
The sea crashing on the rocks.
Boulders crashing down.
Ships out in terrible storm.
An earthquake breaking houses killing people.
Rough sea everywhere.

Robert Finch (9) Princetown CP School

WHEN THUNDER ROLLS

I shiver and shake
When thunder rolls
When the wind whistles past my window
When lightning rips through the sky
It makes me feel like I'm going to cry
Arr! I scream
When thunder rolls.
I dive underneath my cover and try to get to sleep
No use, I say to myself and it's 11.00 pm
I get out of bed,
It's flooded, I cry
Now it's beginning to snow
Then the sun begins to rise and I get to sleep
                                  but it's morning.

Mark Easton (9) Princetown CP School

THE WAR

I see terror I see fright
I see people that need
My help.

I hear gunshots I hear
My heart beat
And my son
Saying
'Help.'

I feel my feelings and
A bad feeling in my
Mind.

Wayne Smith (11) Princetown CP School

HATTIE

Out in the yard there's a dog, galloping
Out in the garden, having fun.
Out in the park, she's making friends
Out on the grass, lying in the sun.

A basset hound, with very long ears
Enormous feet and a wagging tail.
Everywhere, she runs so fast,
Not like a tortoise or a very slow snail.

Honey-brown, with splodges of black
Coffee eyes and paws of white.
She's a very pretty dog,
I love her lots, I hug her tight.

When I come home from school each day,
She runs to me with glee.
Down the steps and into my arms
I shout: *'I'm home, Hattie!'*

Samantha Ingram (11) Princetown CP School

BRIDIE

Bridie is sweet and warm,
She hides herself during a storm,
She runs about,
But only goes out,
If the rain and hail doesn't fall.

She jumps around with glee,
When she's tired she cuddles me,
I blanket her up,
As a cute little pup,
And she dreams of her wonderful tea.

Elizabeth Cronin (11) Princetown CP School

RED

Red is angry red is rage.
Red is the hotness of a hot fire.
Red is as evil as the devils.
Red has the angriness of a raging bull.
Red has the flavour of a hot chilli pepper.
Red has the sound of a pack of raging rhinos.
Red makes the smell of burning rubber.
Red is as red of a bucket of blood.
Red is as red as the sun going down.
When the sun goes down all this red will die.

Andy Routley (11) Princetown CP School

MY HOME

Home is for happiness and sadness.
Home is where I clean my teeth.
Wash my face.
A welcome mat at the back door
I love my home.
Home is special to me.
My home is warm inside
Cold outside.
The lounge is where you sit in front
Of the fire and watching TV too.
Get ready for bed,
Teddy bear welcomes me to bed.
Home is for getting into bed.
All you hear in the night is the
Clock going. Tick, tock, tick, tock.

Home Sweet Home.

Kirsty Masterton (11) Princetown CP School

WARTIME

I feel nice and calm.
I see people talking in the street
I see calm I hear people talking to their friends.

I hear my heart beat fast I hear screams across the street.
I see panic and unkindness and people dead in the street.
I feel cold and scared so I run and hide behind a car in the street.

Craig Liversidge (10) Princetown CP School

KILLERS

Tiger walking without a sound
Keeping close contact with the ground.
Sees a gazelle here and there
Tiger leaps into the air.
Tears out flesh without a care
Now the cubs come for a share.
Come closer if you're a sinner
But the tiger is a dangerous killer.

James Hext-Williams (11) Princetown CP School

WAR!

I see an aeroplane above my head.
I hear the noisy engine of the aeroplane.
I feel my friend hitting me on the head.

I see people running.
I hear people screaming for help.
I feel like I have been shot.

Adrian Roderick (10) Princetown CP School

RED

Red is danger, fear and anger,
It's the colour of velvet roses,
It is also a deep, but deadly strong lipstick,
Red is the colour of the red wine that we all love to drink,
Red is a burn,
And a terrible, but horrible accident,
Red is the colour of strawberries, a cherry, and a red berry
Fruit as juicy as ever,
Red is the deepest part of a chart,
The chart that likes to be in the dark,
It has a very big piece of bark,
It likes to dry with a piece of spark,
The spark is the size of a dart,
And stays up until it is a scary pitch black
Darkness.

Charlotte Finch (11) Princetown CP School

WINTER

Bare trees, no leaves
Snow on the trees
Cold knees
Go inside cup of tea
Put the soup on for tea
Go in sitting room
Sit down looking at my soup - golden - brown
Then I go outside to feed the dogs
Saw some big leaping frogs
Went inside looked outside
Snow melting
I said to myself, 'It's time for bed.'
Went upstairs to rest my head.

Samuel Smerdon (10) Princetown CP School

WAR

I see, happiness.
I hear, laughter, talking.
I feel, warm, relaxed.

I see, panic, terror.
I hear, screams, gunshots.
I feel, scared, worried, helpless, frightened.

Laura Branfield (11) Princetown CP School

WHITE

White is a calm and pretty colour,
Snow is white as white as ever.
White has a beauty no other colour has got,
Silk is a white in a baby's cot.
A furry rabbit's tail,
A beautiful trickling brook.
White is the wind and white is the clouds,
Curling white horses curling in and out.

Lindsey Dunne-Richards (11) Princetown CP School

SOMETHING'S OUT THERE

Something out there, run for help shouting and screaming,
hoping that someone hears.
You hear footsteps behind you so you run faster and faster.
As the noise gets higher and higher.
Then you trip. You see big blue eyes looking down at you.
When your heart starts beating faster and faster as the
gun is held at your head.
Then *Bang!*

Verity Palmer (10) Princetown CP School

WAR

I see happiness in faces,
I hear chattering, laughter, whispers,
I feel relaxed, happy and warm inside.

Suddenly, I see people running for shelter,
Panicking, worried, terror in faces.
I don't hear happiness anymore,
I hear gunshots, hearts thumping,
I feel frightened, worried. I think to myself what's going to happen to my life?

Gemma Beere (11) Princetown CP School

HOMELESSNESS

Cold, wet and grey
I lie in dismay.
I sit alone, nothing to do, a tear in my eye,
But I know someday help will pass by.
I huddle up tight with my clothes which are rags,
A woman walks past with shopping bags.
She stares at me and gives a weak smile,
I smile back for a while.
She walks on past, I give a sigh,
Sometimes I wish I would die.
My stomach tightens, I close my eyes,
But nobody else passes by.

Laura Rattlidge (11) Rydon CP School

HOMELESSNESS

Wet, cold and damp,
I sit huddled up with a painful cramp,
I think about the good old days,
Running away has some bad ways,
The bridge shelters me from the pouring rain,
As I sit thinking in an unknown pain,
The blanket doesn't make me warm,
Because it's shredded, ripped and torn,
I wish I was back home by the fire,
With this thought I try to sleep but I know it will never happen.

Sarah Langley (11) Rydon CP School

HOMELESSNESS

Dirty and skinny,
He sits there every day,
Hungry and thirsty,
No-one ever pays,
He begs for money,
But doesn't get a cent,
And in his heart lies a great big dent.

He has to have money,
He needs some food to eat,
He knows he'll die if he doesn't,
So there lies a hat at his feet,
The generosity of one person, fills the dent in his heart,
And he starts collecting, for a very special treat.

Mark Russell (11) Rydon CP School

HOMELESSNESS

I sit down in my place,
I take my hat off and put it down on the platform of the subway,
The wind is blowing,
Slowly a noise comes from one end of the tunnel,
It gets louder and louder it stops,
All I can see are people's legs rushing by,
Then someone stops they look at me,
She gets a pound out of her purse,
I thank them,
They go quickly and quietly,
They all have gone leaving me all alone,
I got outside and a cool breeze goes down my back.
I hold a picture in my hands,
It's of a girl, the only girl I love, now I'm alone by myself,
I loved my daughter so much,
I said I was sorry it was silly of me to let her
Sit in the front of the car,
It wasn't my fault she died,
I'm scared so much and that's why I moved.

Abby Humphreys (11) Rydon CP School

SEVEN WAYS OF LOOKING AT MAGIC

Quick twist of the hand.
Twist of the mind.
Invisible to eye.
Invisible to brain.
The missing link.
The mystical words
The magic wand.

Richard Matthews (11) Rydon CP School

A HOMELESS MAN

A man, a nobody day-dreaming, wandering
through a strange land with no friends and no
family.

A man, a nobody, scared, afraid, with
nothing to love and no-one to care.

A man, a nobody, remembering how much
he loved to have a warm bath.

A man, a nobody thinking about his
dead family up in safe heaven mourning
over them.

A man, a nobody a stranger to himself he
wished he was home but the memory
is too hard.

A man, a nobody he wants his family
back he wants them back for good to
stay with him forever.

Hannah Sherwood (11) Rydon CP School

PIGS

I love pigs.
They're my favourite animals.
I've got lots of piggy things
In my bedroom
Oink oink!
Pink is my favourite colour
Oink oink!

Zoe Stokes-Davies (8) Rydon CP School

HOMELESSNESS

As I sit here thinking about the life I used to have,
I think about my family and the friends I knew in college.
I feel quite sad when I think of these people because I will
                                           never see them again.

As I think about the home I had before I came to sit here,
I think what a happy place it was with my children running around.
I feel very sad when I think of my children because I will never
                                                         see them again.

As I think about the wife I loved when I had a happy home,
I think of the wonderful smile she gave me before I went to work.
I feel really sad when I think of my wife because I will never see her again.

As I sit here I think how I will get my next meal,
I think how thirsty, starving, cold and lonely I am.
I am not sad when I think of these things because if I die I will not be missed.

I am lying here now dying from thirst and hunger,
I know I will die very shortly because I have no money and I'm too
                                                                   weak to walk.
I will now say goodbye to everyone and everything I knew.

                Goodbye . . .

Emma Webster (10) Rydon CP School

A DAY IN THE LIFE OF A HOMELESS PERSON

I wake up scared, lonely and afraid,
I get out of a box or sometimes not even that,
People laughing, staring and running,
I get up and walk around, I don't want to be homeless,
All day every day I think about my family,
Wishing one day maybe I could live and see them again.

Darren Morrell (11) Rydon CP School

HOMELESSNESS

Are they cold?
Are they sad?
Why are they homeless?
Did he run away from a cold family?
Or wasn't wanted?
Nobody knows.
And then you see us,
Sheltered, safe, private,
And somewhere to go to,
Where a happy family meets you,
And stays with you,
Forever.

Samantha Thompson (10) Rydon CP School

THE WIND

Howling round the window pane
The wind blows.
Puffing, huffing, a tree goes down
The wind blows.
Umbrellas turning inside out
The wind blows
Will it ever stop?

Emily Birt (8) Rydon CP School

VICTORIANS

Victorian teachers
They are strict alright,
They whack you really hard
With the cane.
Ouch!
Who's talking back there?
Victorian teachers
They're strict alright
See I told you they are.

Cassie Humphreys (8) Rydon CP School

BAD WATER

Soaking my sister,
Making her mad.
Squirting my mum,
She says it's so bad.

My brother is wet,
Soaked by a hosepipe.
Now he's very muddy,
His T-shirt needs a wipe.

Having a water-fight,
At the start of the night.
My mum's around the corner,
Now she's out of sight.

Simon Langley (9) Rydon CP School

MY DOG

Here my dog runs,
Faster faster she really runs.
White and spotty and really
dotty
       and
              black
                      and
                              splodgy.
Running like a
bullet with her red collar
ring
       ding
             like
                    a
                          bell.

Hayley Manning (9) Rydon CP School

WEATHER

Rain is tapping on my window
Splashing puddles down below
People scurrying in the town
Market stalls are empty below
The snow is drifting along the town
Heavy, heavy, down, down, down
Across the market along the walls
Across the field
Around and around
It's landed.

Sarah Shore (8) Rydon CP School

WATER PISTOLS

Water pistols are fun
Skimming stones on the pond
Washing up
Washing up with Mum and Dad
Having a cold drink
Orange
       is
             my
                    favourite
                              drink.

Simone Mulholland (9) Rydon CP School

THE NIGHT

In the night I turn the light
on and outside so I can see
Silverstone in the moonlight
over by the sea and I
can hear the sea
crashing against
the rocks over
by the lighthouse
and it calms
down and
the noise
is all
over.

Dayle Ward (9) Rydon CP School

THE ALIENS

One night
My room filled up
With light.
Suddenly my door
Opened, Aliens
Came in
They're going
To get me
Help!
Phew they're nice.

Craig Harris (9) Rydon CP School

THE BIG SPACESHIP

The *big* spaceship going through
space to mars.
Rolling
        away
                from
                        station
                                five
                        Bang!
                it
        has
landed
        on Mars.
                It is there
                Forever!

Laurence Harvey (9) Rydon CP School

SPACE

Space, it's a big place,
I saw an alien.
Have you been to the place?
I started thinking: Malien, Dalien, Salien.

They didn't make sense,
Neither did I.
The ice-creams were only one pence
But I got a bit in my eye.

It started to sting.
I tried to forget about it
But I couldn't . . . *Ding.*
I know!

Let's go back,
To old mother earth
I'll have my tea,
In the place where I had my birth.

Peter Titt (9) Rydon CP School

MY BROTHER

My brother is such a pain
I can't do anything
When he is around
If I want to go swimming
He starts to moan
And feel sorry for himself,
He hides away in a room
But he doesn't go in his room
He goes in my room!
He gets his own way sometimes
And then he is happy.

Sophie Seymour (10) Rydon CP School

SOLAR SYSTEM

I went up in my spaceship
Way above the earth
The sun was shining bright
But something was going on.

Suddenly I was surrounded
By lots and lots of guns
Bye bye it's time for me to go.

On my way back to earth
Zooming through space
On my way back to earth
There was a tremendous crash
I went flying through my bedroom window
Straight into bed.

Christopher Monk (9) Rydon CP School

ICE BALLOONS

The little worm wriggling
through the marbling frosty
forest, was it really there?
If you put salt on an ice
balloon it looks like thunder
and lightning and an earthquake.
Snap, crackle and pop Santa's
Grotto as the elves work inside.
Salty watered ice balloon making
your hands and fingers itch. The
gleaming crystals trying to get
out. Is it a dream or are they
true?

Victoria Elliott & Katie Sneap (8) Rydon CP School

SUMMER'S HERE

Summer's here spring's
behind, birds are in
the trees singing
in the summer
breeze.

        Squirrels are looking
        for nuts again because
        the summer's sunshine
        is sending a
        message all around.

It goes
through the
trees and
under water
and everywhere.

Ryan R Stansfield (8) Rydon CP School

SCHOOL AGAIN

I woke up this morning
And the rain was pouring
I got dressed and made my bed
I went downstairs
To have my breakfast
But my brother had eaten it
So I had dry bread
Off to school
For another boring day.
I can tell when it's going to be boring
Because *my brother's*
Eaten my breakfast!

Jean-Paul Norris (10) Rydon CP School

CRYSTAL BALL

When we put the salt on it went crackle pop,
crackle, crackle, crackle and I thought
it would never stop.
When I felt it, it felt cold and smooth,
the little tiny feathery bits -
well they didn't move.
When we shone the torch on it,
it looked like Santa's grotto,
tiny little pearls that I could see,
it looked like a huge snowball,
that was pretty and round,
standing still so perfectly,
it didn't make a sound.
The little spiky bits reminded me of
a tiny curled up hedgehog,
that stood still,
it looked like a still log.
But now the time has ended
they have crumbled up,
goodbye balloon!

Hannah Bray & Lisa Ward (8) Rydon CP School

HELPING

        Miss *H*emmings and
   Mrs Passmor*E* helps me with reading
Miss Hemmings he*L*ps me with spellings
         I hel*P* with tidying the room
    and all the ch*I*ldren help
   with the tidyi*N*g up
        *G*reat now we can go home.

Paul Tomlinson (10) Rydon CP School

BUBBLE BALL

Floating iceberg on freezing water,
we put the salt on snap, crackle, pop,
thunder, lightning, it made my ear ache,
inside the crystal is my huge snowball.
Frozen crystalball, marble ball, I never can stop looking at it.
It is so beautiful.
Frozen little worm. Trying to reach the air trapped in a cool
cold place. When I look in at the snowball it reminds me
of a snowstorm.
When we put the fizzing salt on rivers started to appear
on the pearl ball.
Lovely crackling rivers.
When I went home I couldn't stop thinking about it. The
Next morning it was gone. I knew it wouldn't last our adventurous
ball. I wish I'll see you again one day.

Natasha Sellick & Joanna Higgins (8) Rydon CP School

KIT CAR

Yes!
Today I hit the highway with the wind in my face
I've got a turbo boosted engine
and I am going in a race.
You can smell the burning rubber
as I am skidding through the bends
I'm arriving at the start line
Off we go
Over in a second
What a show.
I have won the trophy in the end
and for now home again.

Darren Catchpole (10) Rydon CP School

ROLLER BLADES

Zoom
I go whizzing
down the road at top speed.
I'm getting closer
and closer
to the ramp every second.
The wheels are going so fast
you can hardly see them.
I'm heading towards the ramp.
Whizz
I'm in the air now
I do a three sixty
and land on two feet!
I slow down and stop.
I wait for the judges to decide.
Who is going to win the competition?
The judge calls my name out
I lift up the trophy.

Tom Teague (10) Rydon CP School

SPLASHING DOLPHINS

Splashing around in the sparkling sea,
Somersaulting in the air,
Jumping in the blue wake,
The people on the ship say,
'Ooh! What's that beautiful thing down there?'

Blue, bending, diving into the sea,
Showing its top fin while it swims underwater,
Squealing loudly like a whistle,
Speeding like an Olympic swimmer.

I walk across the deck and look down at the dolphins,
They squeal at me and look happy.
I would like to swim with them at the edge of the beach,
It would make me happy.

Liam Mugford (10) Rydon CP School

MY BIG HAMSTER

I am a poor hamster
My eye keeps getting stuck together
But it doesn't matter now
Oh well here I go in my wheel
Round and round and round
I will get a drink now
Gulp, gulp, gulp
I will go up my tube now
Whoops I fell down my tube
I will eat some yummy apple now
Mmmm it's nice and juicy
I will go on my see-saw now
Up and down up and down
I will go in my racing car
Brum, brum, brum
As my feet pedal in my wheel
Goody she is getting me out of my cage
Ow don't squeeze me
Yes she is giving me a cookie
Munch, munch, munch
Oh no she is putting me back in my cage
It doesn't matter I will chew the bar
Oh no I can't get out
Oh well I will go to sleep and have a rest
Zzzzzzzzzzzzzzzzzzzzzzz.

Amanda Davis (9) Rydon CP School

THE POOR IGUANA

A poor iguana slithering in its cage,
At the owner's house,
Waiting for its tail to drag along behind it,
The iguana wishes it was a chameleon,
So it can change colour to hide,
People think it is a horrible creature,
But I like it still,
The iguana likes it when it gets to play with people,
It likes to sit on people's shoulders,
I like the iguana when they get treated well,
But I think it's cruel when they get treated badly,
If I was an iguana and I was treated badly I would try to tell my owners,
This is what he has for his meal:
Some nice, fresh vegetables
And some clean water to drink,
I would like that if I was an iguana,
Its exercise is to run around on the carpet,
If I was allowed I would like an iguana,
But I'm not allowed to because they grow too big,
My dad says I would have to clean him out,
But I wouldn't have time because I'm always out,
I wish he could go faster but if I make him he'll hurt me,
I'd better not try it just in case he does,
But it probably won't hurt,
How come they are slow?
I wonder, I wonder,

Nicola Thomas (10) Rydon CP School

MY LITTLE HAMSTER

Waking up, *yawn*
Getting in the wheel
Start pedalling, start pedalling
Whizzing round, whizzing round
Slowing down
    Stop
Getting off
Climbing the stairs
Now I'm there at the top
Chewing the bars
Let me out,
Climbing the bars
Upside down
Running
    down
        the
            stairs
To his water
Then to his food
Crunch, crunch
Chewing his food
Storing it in his pouch
Walking back to his house
Curling up in a ball, closing his eyes
He's asleep! Zzzzzzzzzzzzzzz.

Sarah Lowe (9) Rydon CP School

CATS

I have 5 cats
They are called
1 Sindy
2 Chloe
3 Jess
4 Ginger
5 Millie
Millie is the youngest
She is 3 months old
Sindy is the oldest
But I don't know how old she is
Cats are soft, hairy, cuddly
I like cats
Sindy is a big cat
She is black white and brown
Chloe is a skinny cat
She is lots of colours
Jess is a mother she has had 4 kittens
And is pregnant at the moment
Ginger is a big cuddly cat
He is a ginger colour
And Millie is a little black cat
I like cats.

Tina Sneap (10) Rydon CP School

THE SKILLS OF THE BEST GAME

Here they come
charging for the away side.
Crash boom bang.
The first tackle is made
it's a very hard one.
It has gone down to the wing.
The crowd are going wild.
Gillespie has crossed it to Ferdinand.
We all know he's got a great header.
But can he do it now?
Yes he can.
The first time in British history.
They think it's all over
it is now.
Albert has just scored a cracker.
A few minutes to go.
Weeeeeeeeeeeeeeeeeeeeeeeeep.

Robert Law (10) Rydon CP School

WWF

It is the heavyweight champion Shawn Micheals
His opponent *Big Van Vader*
Ding ding ding
The match starts
Vader hammering away at Shawn
Shawn's gone down to the canvas
Vader's going to do the *Vader* bomb
He misses
They are both down on the canvas
Diesiel's coming down to the ringside
He tries to get Shawn's attention
But Shawn takes no attention
Vader gets Shawn where it hurts
Shawn goes down
Vader gets to the top rope
He does the *Vader* bomb
He lands right on top of Shawn
Then 1 . . . 2 . . . 3
Vader is the heavyweight champion.

Daniel Jones (10) Rydon CP School

RIVER POEM

Rivers are flowing, down it bounds.
In and around, in and around.
Very fast, very slow.
Every day it's high and low.
Round lots of bends and over a bump.
Past a camel with a hump.
Rapids flowing very fast,
Some water splashes at the mast.
A fish jumps out and looks at me.
Hurray hurray here's the sea.

Charlotte Simkins (9) St Andrew's Primary School, Buckland Monachorum

FLYING

Through my dreams I'd love to fly,
I lose my mind as I soar so high,
over houses the town is far behind me,
dipping and weaving through hill and valley,
I pause a while to hover and float,
oh, elation and joy as I ponder and gloat,
how lucky I am to lose my mind
while I sleep and dream until morning time.

John Beaty (9) St Paul's RC Primary School, St Budeaux

I HAD A LITTLE FISH

I had a little fish
That lived in a dish
Not far away from the sea
I told it once
I told it twice
When can we have our tea?
Flip the fish said you will have to wait
Until it gets to half past eight
We heard a noise
We heard it twice
Then up appeared a dish of mice.

Hayley Squires (9) St Paul's RC Primary School, St Budeaux

BOATS

Splashing and crashing,
In the water they are dashing,
The waves go up and over,
We can see Dover,
All the seagulls land on the boat,
We are wearing our floats,
We will soon be ashore,
Can't wait for some more.

Simon Gilley (9) St Paul's RC Primary School, St Budeaux

DUSK TO DAWN

As the light begins to fade
The gardener puts away his spade
The birds fly to their nests
And children take off their vests.

Windows and doors slam shut
The mouse scampers round for a nut.
And the moths dance in the light
But beware of the animals of the night.

The bats swoop as quiet as can be
Even though they cannot see
Watch out moths the bats can hear
If I were you I'd fly in fear.

Twit-Twoo! Twit-Twoo!
Run little mice he can see you
The tawny owl hoots from the sky
Quick, quick hide as he passes you by.

As the sun starts to appear
The animals of the night disappear
And day begins to reign
And the day starts all over again.

Leanne Lane (9) St Paul's RC Primary School, St Budeaux

HOLIDAY

Holiday holiday don't go away.
O dear got to go.
Lovely food chips chips and, more.
Interesting things to see.
Drip drop your ice-cream melts.
And a beautiful silky sun.
Yes your lovely sunny suntan.
Silky salty sea.
        Sea,
                sea,
                        sea.

Carmen Jarvis (9) St Paul's RC Primary School, St Budeaux

HOLIDAY

Hot warm holidays that's my kind of holiday.
Oh no! My ice-cream's melting it still looks scrumptious.
      So I'll eat it anyway.
Looking for a nice cold drink to cool myself down.
I'm enjoying every little bit of all my time here.
Dreaming of a long cool swim so I rush to get my gear.
All day sunbathing on a very hot beach.
Yet I suppose there's still no place like home.

Nicola McGerty (9) St Paul's RC Primary School, St Budeaux

THE BLACKSMITH

An old man is sitting on a three-legged stool,
The kind used for milking.
He's wearing a shabby brown and green cap,
A pair of moth-eaten shorts and a passed-down shirt.
Using his birchwood, bone-handled walking-stick,
He makes his way with some difficulty over to the fire.
He screws up the paper and throws it into the grate.
He puts a lighted match to the paper.
It flares up and he piles coals on top.
They begin to turn to ash.
The old man picks up a slab of very heavy metal,
And starts to melt it.
Outside four impatient horses are being tied
To the iron rings in the wall by the blacksmith's son.
A cold draught creeps through the gaps in the wood;
The old man hunches himself into a sheepskin coat.
He begins to hammer the metal into shape.
He carefully shoes the horses.
The old man damps his white hair and beard,
And mops his aged brow.

Emily Hawkins (10) South Brent Primary School

SWEET TOOTH'S HEAVEN

The caramel caresses carelessly in my cavities,
Jelly-tots jumping in my jaws.
My toffee tumbles tantalisingly in my tummy,
Sticky substance on my paws!

Flavour comes frolicking out of fruit pastilles,
Jumping out of jellybeans,
Juju-bean juices trickling down my throat,
Oh, I love peppermint creams!

Alice Holland (10) South Brent Primary School

UNTITLED

P eople are welcome to visit.
E veryone will have a good time.
N o dangers ahead or behind.
S ome bugs are there in the trees and on the leaves.
T oads and frogs live in little bogs.
A nd water plants live in streams.
V ery nice views.
E very spring everything goes its own colour.

C heeping from chicks fill the air.
O pen to anyone.
P lease come along say the animals,
S till there's a stillness about it all.
E nchanting.

Merin Cox-Davies (10) South Brent Primary School

LAND OF ANAKA

People crying out for help
Driven from their own country
Not knowing where to go
Their hopes and dreams were shattered
Their crops did not grow.
They have nothing to remember
Their happy past life by.
Nothing is left, everything is gone!
Horrible and cruel people drive
Others from their homes.
Now the same cruel people are left
To rule a deserted but once
Beautiful, happy, colourful land.
Everything is gone.
      Destroyed.

Rebecca Pitts (11) South Brent Primary School

THE GHOSTLY NIGHTMARE

I went upstairs and got into my bed
A slimy thing touched my head
I gasped and cried
And screamed and sighed
And then the nightmare struck.

The ghost flew past by me
And then I did see
A head in the cupboard
The body behind
You'd never guess what else I did find.

The bed was drenched with vomit
My hair dyed yellow and green
And then the worst thing I had ever seen
A witch on her broomstick
With the cat in the pot.

I wish my nightmare was over
And then I would never have seen
All the gruesome, horrible
Disgusting things
That had been.

Laura Pitts (10) South Brent Primary School

A MAN FROM BERLIN

There was a fat man from Berlin
Who wanted to live in a bin
He got stuck when he went to try it
So he went on a crash diet
And now he's awfully thin.

Maxine Valpy (10) Stoke Hill Middle School

CAMP

Dear James
What is this food bad get yourself
together lad. Want more money is
this a joke for all we care you can
choke. We have seen your bedroom
it's a terrible mess when it comes to
money you will get less. Sick on
coach why not in loo when you get
back will surely sue. I'll see you soon
my love you do know you're my little
dove.

Adam Bishop (10) Stoke Hill Middle School

POLLUTION

Pollution in the sea,
pollution in the air.
With empty cans of coke,
pollution is everywhere.

Pollution is horrid,
pollution is gross.
Pollution shouldn't be here
and that ain't no joke!

Pollution shouldn't be here
and that is really true.
I try to keep the world clean
now why don't you?

David Vernon (10) Stoke Hill Middle School

PLAY TIME

Susie Loony eating flies
Lisa joyfully flies kites
David Poom makes lots of pooms
Henry Firsty is very firsty.

Amy Dought said I doubt it very much
Lucky and Chris are playing kiss-chase
Christopher and Barrie playing football
Lisa and Nasra playing netball.

Adam and Colleen kissing the playground
Laura and Chrispy are making love
Simon and Andy are being gay
Emma and Heather writing things down.

Jon and Andrew up the tree
Amy and Maxine are speaking about Michael
Bret is watching other people
Kristy is playing pogs.

Sheradon is cheating on pogs
James Berryman is doing gym
Kyle is on the toilet
Tamsyn and Chris are picking their nose.

Lucky and Leanne are doing drawings
Colleen and Laura are showing off
And Colleen was worrying about her jewellery
Amy had curly hair.

Leanne Rose (9) Stoke Hill Middle School

MY EXCITING HOLIDAY

We went to Doniford Bay
The chalet we stayed in was cosy.
The five days we were there
We never had a moment to spare.

We had pirates ahoy and swimming
Every single day.
Go-Karts and bumper boats I liked best
I would not need a rest.

Pirate's ahoy had lots of rope ladders
It was shaped like an enchanted ship
Then I went on the water slide
What an exciting ride!

My sister and I shared a room
And we all had a go to sleep on the couch
My mum and dad watched us play
Over-looking the rocky bay.

Haven holiday we will never forget
With all the fun we had.
One thing's for sure, whatever the weather
I could have stayed there forever.

Nasra Al-Hashmi (10) Stoke Hill Middle School

THE TRAMP

He sits in the doorway,
A lonely figure,
Dishevelled and grimy,
His head bowed down,
He begs for small change,
He's not wanted in this town,

People glance at him,
Then rush past,
No time to worry about him,
Must get home on a cold winter's night,
But there's no home for him,
Is this right?

Andy Bartlett (10) Stoke Hill Middle School

MORNING BREAK

People come out shouting
Michael gets the goal
Andy comes out with the ball trips all over Paul

Adam stays out picking his nose and stores it in his clothes
Ben swears when he's eating pears and
Simon swallows slugs

Mrs Trolly is a wally when she's eating holly.
Peter slate broke a plate on his way to dinner.

What a lot of nonsense during morning break!

Michael Kevin Crump (10) Stoke Hill Middle School

FAIRY

When I climb on a horse,
It usually is Fairy,
She's a bay with a white blaze,
I stroke her mane it's hairy.

Heels down, shorten reins,
Start to trot.
Up, down, up, down,
I love it a lot,

Prepare to canter
A wonderful gait,
I kick her on,
Both of us can't wait.

Suddenly Fairy bolted,
Galloping around,
Then she stopped,
I hit the ground.

I got back on
Are you OK?
Was it fast?
They all began to say,

After I answered all their questions
We did a perfect jump,
Then we went in and I gave her a pat,
And a sugar lump.

Emma Ridgeon (10) Stoke Hill Middle School

THE WORLD

The world is full of dangers
Every country has one
What are we doing destroying
The world.

Volcanoes snakes and creatures
Are all dangers to us
We have not been caring
So why are we here?

Why hasn't God
Done anything to the
World it is probably
For us to sort something out.

But governments are
Not helping us
Plants trees and animals
We cannot kill them

The world is a place
Of terror at every corner
Everywhere.

Sheridan Ingram (10) Stoke Hill Middle School

MORNING BREAK

Chuckie looks like a hockey puck
Phil and Lill have to have a
funny pill, Amie and Maxie playing
basket ball against the wall.

Gill became very ill, Heather really likes
Space and so does Sarah Slace
Emma Ridgeon is a big fan of
Pidgeons, and Coll plays with
her dolls.

Amie Ormand (10) Stoke Hill Middle School

WHAT I THINK OF OUR ENVIRONMENT

Our environment isn't what I'd like,
Holes in the ozone layer because
Of aerosol spray.
Rubbish and litter all over the place
Because even though there's bins
People don't use them
Can't everyone do something is
this really what we want?

Trees are being chopped down
Because we can't recycle
Whole rainforests disappearing just
to have a seat.
Can't everyone do something is this
really what we want?

Charlotte Stephens (10) The Grove School

A SLAVE'S WORLD TO ME

A slave's world is cold and dark
But their hopes never die.
Chains belonging to someone else wrapped around their hands,
Chains that have been worn time and time again.

A slave would be lucky if they were given a slice of bread to eat,
or get more than one piece of
cloth to wear.
Do these people have a life or is it run by others?
No-one knows what they must be feeling but we can try to understand,
They must be sad, and sadness is . . .
Slow, stiff and low,
It's cold like snow.
It's as big as a face, but the face is a face of a different race.
Someone with a different skin colour, someone with different views,
morals,
But no less of a person than us, just different.
Someone slow,
Someone low,
Someone's freedom is gone,
Someone's sadness.

Victoria Blake (9) The Grove School

THE KOALA

I saw a koala that ran up a tree
It was very very frightened of me
She had a baby on her back
Which went smack, smack, smack,
Smack, smack, smack.

She twitched her nose and gave a smile,
And then looked back in a while
She climbed up the very big tree
Without a scratch from her flea!

She ate a leaf from the very big tree,
And then her baby bounced on her knee
Oh mummy he said I'm having such fun
Up here in the tree eating the gum

No my dear the koala said
We have to go back into our bed
We have to go down very very deep
To lie in our bed and go to sleep.

Lindsay Bishop (10) The Grove School

SLAVES

Cold and lonely
Dark and sad
Slaves don't know how to play
All they do is work all day.

I've often thought how horrible
It must be to be a slave,
They must wish to be so free,
Free as a bird.

They must wish with all their might
To spread their wings and fly
Not to be slaves slaves slaves . . .

Pennie Lamkin (10) The Grove School

SIR FRANCIS DRAKE

When Francis Drake was young
His voyage had begun
He went to sea
And was very happy
Because his journey was going to be fun.

He thought it was best
To sail to the west.
The Spaniards were there
But he didn't care
And stole their treasure chests.

On the Golden Hind
He made up his mind
To sail far and wide
Carried by the tide.

The weather man had lied
It was too hot to glide
They thought they oughta
get some water
before the all died.

They came home after four years
everyone was in tears.
He was knighted by the Queen
Because of the jewels she had seen.

Sarah Harrison (10) Tidcombe Primary School

SIR FRANCIS DRAKE

The rap that I'll tell you,
Is about this fellow brave and true,
His name was Sir Francis Drake,
As a sailor he was no fake,

He read a map at ease,
And his ship mates were all too pleased
Many places, many wars,
Many adventures, many abhor!

Like the time they had a stormy ride,
On an island - wrecked ships they hide,
Tired of the global tour,
He returned to England safe once more,

The Queen she knighted him, and said,
'Francis Drake, dear old thing,
The Spanish King he wants a fight,
Go and deal with all your might.'

He fought the Spaniards brave and true,
He ransacked the town and castle too.
The Queen, she gave him a rest,
His life was now at its best.

Then that message came one day,
From the Queen who had to say,
Fight the Spaniards they're back again
Spanish ships were clumsy and slow,
They finished them off! It was time to go.

So in this rap it goes to say,
That Francis Drake is remembered today,
He put the Spanish fleet to shame,
And earned himself undying fame.

Charlotte Brown (10) Tidcombe Primary School

THESUS AND THE MINOTAUR

There was a king called Minos,
Who lived in Crete,
He lived in a castle
With a maze at its feet.

Minos's son went to Athens,
To take part in some sports,
But he was killed so horribly,
What a terrible thought.

Theseus said one day 'Look dad I am going away,
I'm going to kill the Minotaur today.
If I put up a white sail I'm fine,
If I put up a black sail my blood is wine.'

When they got to the maze,
He saw a dark and gloomy haze.
Theseus tied string to the door,
And started to crawl along the floor.

He looked up and saw him face to face,
He turned and stabbed it in the neck,
Then he thought 'Cor bloomin heck'.

Soon they got in the boat and sailed away,
And ended up on a distant bay.
They slept all night and in the morn,
Theseus gave a great big yawn.

When Ariadne was asleep,
He sailed away (what a creep!)
Ageus saw them coming back
then he noticed the sail was black.
He jumped off the rock it was a great shock
Imagine what would happen to poor Theseus.

Rosie Lamb (10) Tidcombe Primary School

THESEUS AND THE MINOTAUR

The King of Crete, Minos was his name.
Sent his son to play, in the Olympic games.
He won a shield,
And then was killed.
King Minos was very mad,
He said the Athenians had been bad.
He sent some ships to attack,
The king of Athens said 'Take them back.'
You must give us seven girls and boys every ninth year,
All the grown ups shed a tear.
Theseus told his dad he was going away,
'I'm going to kill the Minotaur today.
On my return - a white sail says I'm alright,
But a black sail says - I lost the fight.'
So he went to the maze under the palace in Crete.
Where Ariadne fell for him, head over feet.
When it was dark in the middle of the night.
She told him a secret about how to fight.
Take some string.
And this sharp thing.
Now tie the string to the maze door.
And go and find the Minotaur.
He looked the Minotaur in the eye.
And said 'You are greedy, you must die.'
Then he stabbed him in the chest.
And sailed away towards the west.
His dad jumped off a rock.
He couldn't be saved by a Doc.
Because Theseus forgot about the sail.
His dad is dead and that's the end of this tale.

Laura Gratton (10) Tidcombe Primary School

DANIEL IN THE LION'S DEN

Life for Daniel really went down
When the Persian army marched into town.
Persia was really tight. That was why they'd won the fight.

The new king wanted to employ young Dan
Because he thought he was such a clever man.
The king's ministers hated Daniel.
They wanted to send him to hell!

When they watched him pray at work
They thought he was really a jerk!
They offered the king a new law.
Anyone who broke it would face a lion's jaw!

People would ask for help only from his highness.
Otherwise they'd end up as a lionly mess!
Daniel did not want to disobey -
But he still prayed to God every day.

He was thrown in the lion's cave.
Inside he tried to be brave.
The lions roared and growled.
This didn't make Daniel feel proud.

He put his hands together and started to pray.
Religious and holy words he did say.
That night the king couldn't sleep.
Not even by counting sheep.

He couldn't believe this had happened to his friend.
Now he was sure this truly was the end.
In the morning at half past ten,
He walked down to the lion's den.

When rolled back the rock, he had a very big shock!
Daniel came out into the light looking such a normal sight!
Later the king threw the plotters into the den.
But this time . . . *they didn't come out again!*

Peter Byrom (10) Tidcombe Primary School

STAGE FRIGHT

About to go
on
I'm petrified
Couldn't be more
scared
If I tried

I'm going to go on
And sing a song
I can't remember the
second line
Somebody come and
save me . . .

Yes, yes I've remembered
it
It's 'Any day any time'
I'm on now
Singing the song
Oh, no I've done that bit
wrong
Finished at last!

Kimberly Saunders (10) Wembury CP School

MEMORIES OF A WHALE

Leaping high above the waves,
Swimming past the beaching caves.
Graceful, peaceful, humpback whale.

They play in the golden-blue blanket
of sea,
Looking for the silver key.
To open the door of Peace.

Laura Louise Michie (11) Wembury CP School

IMAGINATION ZOO

Imagine, just imagine your very own zoo.
It could have tigers that roar,
And birds that sweep and soar.

You could have an aviary full of owls,
Eagles and more,
And remember your tigers, the tigers that
roar.

You could have a field full of antelopes
That leap and prance,
And even a room, a room full of ants.

An aquarium full of fishes all red, yellow and
white,
And tanks full of snakes that slither and bite.

Imagine, just imagine your very own zoo.
Not in the real world,
But in your dreams, just for you.

Katrina Rae (10) Wembury CP School

BOATS

Down by the river
All boats are bobbing
A canoe
A dinghy

But best of all
Is my little boat
Bobbing down the river
Out of sight
For the night.

Emma Hill (8) Wembury CP School

CHILDREN OF DUNBLANE

Dear little children in heaven tonight,
While your mummies and daddies pray
For you this night,
We all did silence for you my dears but
It did not fled away our tears,
It's so sad dying but don't fear crying
My angels this night.

Carly James (11) Wembury CP School

MORTEHOE GRAVEYARD . . .

The chime of the clock died away, midnight.
The wind howled between the tall grey,
Cracked tomb stones.
Boom! A crash of thunder crashed above the
Graveyard.
Tap-tap, the lock nailed onto the wooden
gate knocked against it.
Bang! Lightning struck the church tower
And a stone dropped to the damp ground
Whoosh, a gust of wind blows the gate
open.
The moon glistened and gave out an
eerie light.
A figure, the ghost of Lady Chichester
Stood by the entrance of the church.
A squeak of a frightened vole echoed
amongst the graves.
A roar of wind bellowed around the village
and the hedges hissed as though vampires
awakening lay among the ivy.
At last the first streak of light dawned on
the graveyard.

Katharine Bond (11) Woolacombe CP School

SEA SOUNDS

The yellow sand glows as the sun shines down.
You hear the wind echo
and whistle through the caves and over pipes.
Splash go the waves against the rocks.
Roar, another wave appears up out of the sea.
ZZZZ here comes the speed boat
Whizzing through the water 'diga diga diga.'
The helicopter flies across the beach
Spreading the golden sand.

Mark Middlemass (10) Woolacombe CP School

OUR COASTLINE

Morte's craggy, angry rocks,
Drift into Woolacombe's smooth untroubled beach.
All made from a thousand grains of gold.
Holiday makers scattered like seeds in the sun.
People run down to frolic in the sea,
As it licks the beach, like a child licking a lollipop,
In turn washing away the people into the night.
They clamber home to dreamy Mortehoe.
Full hotels and comfy beds,
Thinking of the battle of sandcastle and sea.
Aaah! . . . Isn't our coastline beautiful?

Lucy Cansfield (9) Woolacombe CP School

SUMMER FUN IN WOOLACOMBE AND MORTEHOE

The busy village
Is filling up quickly
Full of impatient people
From the village school
You can look out
At the wide stretched ocean
Its waves lapping the golden sand.

Jagged rocks around the point
Filling in the views like a stitch
In a patchwork quilt.

Hills around the bay
Make the patchwork quilt seem so real
With the dark hedges and light green fields
Cows grazing in the fields
Massive herds
Birds singing
Filling in the sound of the sweet day.

I prefer the beach when it is full of holiday makers,
Not when it is lonely and empty.
In summer it is like paradise
Sometimes I think I'm in a different country,
It's so hot.

When you look from the hill of Mortehoe
The view looks so wonderful
It seems like you're in a dream.

Kate Kilner (9) Woolacombe CP School

THE SEA

The sea is rippling over the sandy beach
The cry of a fierce storm is not far away.
As the deep blue sea starts making angry sounds
from the rolling waves.

When the sea calms
Wrecks appear in the gloom of the dark blue sea
New shelter is to be found along the coast.
The storm wears away yet bigger caves
Tangled seaweed gets carried with the still
strong current.

Christopher Smith (11) Widecombe-In-The-Moor School

I ALWAYS GET TOLD OFF

I didn't know there was someone round the corner
When I threw my boomerang
I am always getting told off.

When they shout at me I don't do anything
But I always cry.
I always get told off.

I never get in a mood
Or shout at the teacher
I always get told off.

When I'm really bad
I always go to the head
I always get told off.

Why don't they look at it my way
Or blame someone else
I always get told off.

Mark Andrew Whiteside (11) Widecombe-In-The-Moor School

RHINO

I'm a big black rhino
With a point on my nose
I love to practice ballet
On the tip of my toes
I like to have a doze
In the middle of the day
I snore so much
And my friend run away.

Amanda Whiteside (11) Widecombe-In-The-Moor School

THE KILLER WHALE

It leaps from the water like a jet powered submarine.
Its skin is black and shiny like a wet tyre
His white under body is as pale as the snow
It lives in the dark gloomy water of the sea.

It's like a black and white dragon with teeth
As sharp as swords.

George Adaway (10) Widecombe-In-The-Moor School

SEA THUNDER

Depth of the ocean tide is not a friend of mine.
A shark infested water is what terrifies me.
The ocean bed it carries me away just like
A sea serpent a terrifying creature that lurks in the
Depths. Dull heavy waves of a huge storm brewing.

Oliver Wakeham (10) Widecombe-In-The-Moor School

BEAUTIFUL BEACH

As the ripples of the rock pools go round
and round
Like a whirlpool as it finally crashes
against the rim.

People water-skiing on the luscious clear
blue sea.
Close to the shore and the beach.

Stretching far and wide out of their
depth.
Fish rolling through the green seaweed.

As the sand squelches between my toes
It tickles as the hot sun shimmers across
the sand.

Slowly a gale, a wind forms as I hurry
across the beach, miserable as the golden
sun fades away.

I hope I can go
again some day.

Emma Jones (10) Widecombe-In-The-Moor School

A RIVER IS LIKE . . .

A river is like a
Sparkling crystal
A rushing water slide
A blue sky
A clean swimming pool.

Abigail Faulkner (8) Wolborough C of E Primary School

MY MAGIC BOX

I will give to my mum
The feel of the wind
The sound of birds tweeting in the trees
The noise of the sea.
The touches of silk flowers
The smell of fresh moorland air
The feel of a new born baby
The box will be made out of silk and
A lock made of a bit of my hair
The key will be made of my love

I will give to my dad
A house of glass
The taste of chocolate
The feel of rubber handlebars
The smell of the countryside
The box will be made of paper
With a key made of birds feathers.

Kylie Westaway (9) Wolborough C of E Primary School

MY FAVOURITE PLACE

Sad because before cars
It was quieter and happier
The forest dark but colourful
Grass swaying from side to side
Wind blowing fast and smooth,
The smell of bark so sour but sweet
Morning air so clear and fresh
Glad because I've shared its beauty.

Gina McDermott (9) Wolborough C of E Primary School

MY FAVOURITE PLACE

Peace
Trees rustling
The sunset going down
Red, yellow
A giant ball
Creeping down like a snail
Footsteps, people speaking
I feel carried away
Heart beating
Breathtaking
The rough on the tree
Wet and strong
The smell of people stepping in mud
And the breeze of fresh air.

Daniel Bunclark (9) Wolborough C of E Primary School

MY NAN'S GARDEN

Peace and quiet
Except
Birds singing in the trees
It makes me feel happy
To hear the kids playing
Next door
I just sit on the spiky grass
and relax
The smell of the flowers
Peaceful at 12.30 am
Sunny spring
Flower petals are smooth
Sad when taken away.

Laura Flaherty (9) Wolborough C of E Primary School

DOLPHIN

To make a dolphin
Take a block of gold and mould it in the sun.
To make the skin use some cling-film and wrap it
round the blue moon.
For inside the dolphin's body take the summer wind
of a bright summer's day.
You also need a thunder cloud for the dolphin's
anger when disturbed.
For the dolphin's snout take a cane from a
beanstalk and dip it in the horizon.
Then finally for the loving eyes of the dolphin
take two gems and sprinkle them with sadness.

Katherine Bennett (9) Wolborough C of E Primary School

TIGER

To make a tiger's body
Take a piece of smooth stretchy clay
Shape it in to the slopey strong body
Of a tiger
Cover the clay with a piece of fur
Dipped in the golden sun
Then get a paint brush and dip it
In the night sky
Stroke it down the tiger's body
For the tiger's dark stripes
Inside the body
Put two jet engines for the speed
Then put the crashing waves
Roaring up the rocks
For the tigers fierceness.

Richard Ford (9) Wolborough C of E Primary School

MY MAGIC BOX

I will give my mum
A silk dress with flowers on
A bark of a poodle
A glittered scented candle
I will put them in a box
Made out of snakes' skin
The lock made out of brass
The key made out of roses.

I will give my dad
Sharks running through the sea
After-shave to put under his neck
The touch of a bottle of wine
The feel of the head of a maine-coon
I will put them in a box
Made out of a leather jacket
With spiders legs for hinges
A lock made out of beetles
With a key of worms.

Danielle Palmer (9) Wolborough C of E Primary School

RIVER CHATTER

See the river chatting to itself
Cold and wet flowing down hill
Shiny like a star
The river splashing against the rocks.

Water tinkling under the sun
See it swirling round and round
Look at the twirling wet water
Chatting and tinkling its own language.

Chloe Grove (9) Wolborough C of E Primary School

MY MAGIC PRESENTS

I will give my mum
The noise of thunder and lightning
The smell of a rose
The smell of dumpling stew
The feel of a silk nighty
The walk around Foggintor
I will put these things
In a box made of the sun
A lock of silver
And a key made of love.

I will give Kylie
A horse and cart
The smell of chocolate cooking and fudge
The feel of water
A ride on a horse on the moors
I will put these things
In a box made of chocolate
A lock of love
And a key made of red ribbon.

Emma Westaway (9) Wolborough C of E Primary School

A RIVER IS LIKE

A river is like a straw
A river is like a rope
A river is like a road
A river is like a main road
A river is like a gleaming snake
A river is like a pencil
A river is like a silver snake.

Thomas Raes (9) Wolborough C of E Primary School

MY MAGIC BOX

I would give my mum
A dog that turns back into
a puppy
A touch of a lion
The sound of water smacking
against boats
The sound of the trees
Rustling in the wind
Roast cooking in the cooker
I would give my mum
the feel of the animals
and birds.
I would give my mum
The power of a lion.

Billie Bowers (9) Wolborough C of E Primary School

MY MAGIC BOX

I will give my mum
The sound of the sea smashing together
The pal of the wind blowing gently
The smell of clean fresh children and after-shave
The feel of plasticine
The touch of a lovely smooth gentle parrot
All coloured and bright
The smell of her strong perfume
The taste of orange juice
The box will be made of ruby and diamonds
The key would be made of crystal and glitter
The hinges will be made from shining stars.

Sam L Faulkner (9) Wolborough C of E Primary School

MY MAGIC BOX

I will give my mum
The sound of the gentle wind blowing
The smell of magnolia perfume
Poured over silky yellow roses
A flamingo
With its brightly coloured feathers
Standing in the water
Balancing on one leg
The sun rising
Oranges and reds glowing
I would make the box out of
Sparkling white crystals
The hinges made of suede
The key made out of liquidized chocolate
The lock made out of black shiny velvet
I would put the silky yellow roses
Round the crystal box.

Angela Gilding (9) Wolborough C of E Primary School

BOMBING

I'm in an Anderson Shelter
I see lights flashing in the sky
I hear bombs exploding
I smell the gas
I cuddle up
I feel worried
I'm terrified
Are you?

Heather Smith (9) Wolborough C of E Primary School

MY MAGIC BOX

To mum I would give
The sound of panting runners
The smell of the Cornish sea
The paw of every dog now living
The World.

The box will be made out of animals
The hinges of tigers' teeth
The key out of a dog's howl.

To Dad,
The height of Snowdonia
The smell of a cold Canadian winter
The taste of icy cold water
The touch of snow he's so used to.

The box will be made of Wales
The hinges of Glamorgan
The lock of Port Talbot.

I would give to my brother
The touch of cheekiness
The might of the Gladiators
The spirit of Linford Chrisitie
The feel of being a real soccer star.

The box will be made of soccer
The hinges of Liverpool
The key of Steve McManaman.

Mathew Rowlands   (9) Wolborough C of E Primary School

MY MAGIC BOX

I will give my mummy a noise like the sea
The feel of the wind
The smell of a roast dinner
A soft kitten on her lap
The feel of a baby's face
Smoother than a pebble
I will put it in a box of love and happiness
With a lock of a rose
And a key of diamonds.

I will give to Dad
The noise of a new drill
The feel of whiskers on his face
The smell of oil
The taste of clotted cream
I will put in a box of liquorice allsorts
With a lock of shiny screws
And a key of cement.

Hannah Wickens (9) Wolborough C of E Primary School

A RIVER IS . . .

A river is like a long motorway.
A river is like a long silver pipe.
A river is like a gurgling monster.
The river is clean like tap water.
A river is like a tiger's growl.
A river is like a long piece of paper.
A river is like a long blue leg.
A river is like a piece of paint.

Louis Phelps (8) Wolborough C of E Primary School

AUTUMN

Bleak mist darker
My grandad grows cabbages
Apples are juicy mouth-watering
Wetter damp bleak
Roast chicken as white as a feather
Acorns green yellow hard like jacks
Wizzy brown helicopters
Red conkers coming down
Mushroom like white umbrellas
Cosy inside by the fire
On the settee
Nice and warm.

Liam Clutsam (9) Wolborough CE Primary School

A RIVER IS ...

A river is a tumble dryer
A sink or a washer
A river is a hill, undulating down
A river is a whirlpool, swirling over stones
A river is a pot of ink, swirling round and round
A river can be anything, because really nobody cares.

A river is a long, long meadow
Flowered with corn and barley
A river is a long, long motorway, with long hours from
cars thumping and smacking his back, a river is like a long piece
of tinsel sparkling by the fire
A river is like a second hand watch
Waiting for someone to buy him.

Chloe Edgeley (9) Wolborough C of E Primary School

A RIVER IS LIKE ...

A river is like a
Silver chain
A pretty silver chain
        A river is like a
        long motorway
        A long busy motorway.
A river is like a long
piece of tinsel
A sparkling long piece
of tinsel.
        A river is like a
        long washing-line
        A long hanging washing
        line.
A river is like a long
jungle
A long fearsome jungle.
        A river is like a
        long thermometer
        A long hot thermometer
A river is like an
unrolled ball of string
A long woolly ball of string.
        A river is like a long
        flower's stem
        A long golden flower's
        stem.

Fiona Walton (8) Wolborough C of E Primary School

SILVER SNAKE

Silver rivers bending
Ivy rivers climbing hills
Lively gurgling noises
Violets grow beside a twinkling river
Ever twisting and bending is a river
Rivers are swooshing and whooshing.

Silver snake river gleaming and glinting
Never does a river stop
A river falls down a waterfall
Kicking and smacking the river gets bigger
Ever and ever runs a river with a twinkle
      In its eye.

Amy Blackmore (8) Wolborough C of E Primary School

IN MY CAULDRON

In my cauldron
I have a
spell
with
lizard legs
pig legs
it chisels
and bezels
and whizels
there's
eyeballs
and frogs
and bugs
and slugs
then pop
it disappears.

Ben Herd (8) Wolborough C of E Primary School

A RIVER IS LIKE . . .

A river is like a silver chain
A river is like a wiggly worm
A river is like a piece of tinsel
A river is like a gurgling sink
A river is like a piece of white fishing line.

Sam Stokoe (8) Wolborough C of E Primary School

A RIVER IS LIKE . . .

A river is like a silver chain.
A river is like a silver pencil.
A river is like a long piece of glass.
A river is like a bit of Sellotape.

A river is like a silver chain.
A river is like a bendy piece of plastic.
A river is like a silver piece of toothpaste.
A river is like a silver crayon.

A river is like a silver wire.
A river is like a long line of paint.
A river is like a silver pen.
A river is like a golden thread.

Lisa Collins (8) Wolborough C of E Primary School

THE SEA

Sometimes when I go down to the sea
I hear it whooshing,
the waves crash together and clash
and sometimes they splash.

I like to swim and paddle.
I like it when the waves
splash, clash and crash.

Jacqueline Smith (9) Woodford Junior School

A SMALL GREY DOLPHIN

A small grey dolphin
looked up at me,
his tale swishing
in the grey blue sea.
I wonder what he's thinking,
I wonder how he feels?
Do you like other fish,
or do you like the eels?

Kathryn Greer (8) Woodford Junior School

MONOPOLY

My brother and I play Monopoly,
He always cheats, then wins,
He never goes to jail,
But visits when I'm in!

Once he bought Vine Street,
And I had to pay sixteen pounds if I landed on it,
Then he bought Mayfair,
And I thought time to quit!

But today I'm the banker,
It'll be me who cheats,
I'll give him what for,
He won't forget it for weeks!

Two hundred pounds you collect,
When you pass go,
To even the score,
I collected more!

I bought Old Kent and White Chapel Road,
Which he thought was funny,
With hotels on,
He had to part with his money.

He landed on Chance,
And was fined on all his properties,
I knew by then,
I was bringing him to his knees.

Landing on White Chapel Road,
For the second time,
Four hundred and fifty pounds, the rent,
Now the game was mine!

Kimberley Moses (9) Woodford Junior School

MY FLOWER

The sun does shine,
and the rain does fall,
My flower grew big
big and tall
big and tall,
but started off so little and small.
The seed split open
a stem grew up
leaves came open
and leaves grew up.
The stem grew taller, really high up
and last came the bluebells
like tiny cups.
The tiny balls that grew inside
looked at me with so much pride.
This is the story of how bluebells grew,
See you next time when I grow some a new.

Jodie Clamp (7) Woodford Junior School

THE SILLY MAN

He eats rotten apples.
He eats poisonous pens.
He loves the smell of garbage,
And the hay of chicks and hens.

He never brushes his smelly hair.
He hates the smell of a rose.
He really is a silly man,
                      . . . I suppose.

Lucy Ellis (9) Woodford Junior School

SCHOOL DINNERS . . .

School dinners Yuk!
Lumpy custard,
Mushy green cabbages.
Carrots that stick out like rabbits' ears.
The cook saying every day 'What do you want my dear?'
Spaghetti that looks like a worm from a hole.
A sign that says join the lunch bunch.
I say to myself why oh why can't I be,
packed lunch.

Nicholas Harris (9) Woodford Junior School

ORANGE

Orange is for orange, all juicy and sweet.
Orange is for autumn leaves, crunching under my feet.
Orange is for the setting sun on the horizon afar.
Orange is for a tiger, with his stripes of camouflage bar.
Orange is for a flame with flickers of orange light.
Orange is for the birdwing butterfly, fluttering through the
                                        rainforest bright.
Orange is for the swordtail fish swimming in a swirling river.
Orange is for the parrots' feathers all in a quiver.

Richard Lake (10) Woodford Junior School

MY CAT

My cat is a black cat
and I love him.
purrrrrr-purrrrrrr
miaow.

But don't dare disturb his slumber
or-he-will-scratch-you.
hissss, hissss
miaow.

Whenever I try writing
he noses my pen
in fact-
he is doing it now
miaow
purrr purrr purrr.

He kisses me in a special way
he loves me lots and lots.
miaow.

Shadow, my cat
he is my special four-legged friend.

When it is time for bed
he curls up by my head.
miaow miaow.

I love him
he loves me
we are both friends,
special friends.

Alex Wright (10) Woodford Junior School

WAVES

Waves can be rough.
Waves can be tough.
When I jump in,
the waves make a fuss.
It is very tumbly,
and very jumbly,
in the sea.

Paula Anderson (8) Woodford Junior School

THE FAIRY POEM

Once I saw a fairy sitting in a tree,
Making daisy chains as quiet as can be.

Early in the morning, with her magic touch,
Sprinkling the flowers that we love so much.

I saw a lady watering the plants,
then she caught me frightening off the ants.

Samantha MacDougall (9) Woodford Junior School

BROOMSTICK

Broomstick, broomstick make me fly!
Make me fly into the sky!
Sky sky make me fly!
Make me fly into the eye!
Eye eye make me fly!
Make me fly back in the sky!

Natalie Roberts (8) Woodford Junior School

BOUNCING BEARDY

A bouncing fluffy dog,
A bouncing toast eating dribbler,
A bouncing people wetter,
When he shakes.

A bouncing garden destroyer,
A bouncing walk lover,
A playful puppy,
Whose teeth are very sharp.

A sleepy, bouncing, black and white dog,
A bouncing sprinter,
A bouncing tail wagger,
Who's never bad. (Well, almost never)

A bouncing scavenger,
A bouncing sniffer dog,
A bouncing ball chaser.
My best friend.

Stephanie Griggs-Trevarthen (10) Woodlands Park Primary School

LIFESAVERS

I'm drowning, alone.
Nobody to help.
Gulping for air but it's water.
The water is bubbling,
I can feel the waves crashing
My arms thrashing, I can't swim.

A dolphin swims by.
It tries to help but it can't.
The dolphin clicks and moans
More dolphins come to help.
They lift me up
To the surface, they carry me to shore.

I am alive and
On dry land.
I thank the dolphins for being so helpful.
I tell them
We should take more care of the sea and its creatures.

Zoe Baines (10) Woodlands Park Primary School

SECRET EXPRESSIONS

Eyes as round as marbles,
staring down at me.
Looking me all over,
checking, I could see.

The sad expression began to change,
grinning wildly.
Looking strange,
acting really weird.

This expression faded quickly,
when a boy came down the hill.
The picture changed to normal,
as if nothing happened at all.

Ashleigh Goddard (10) Woodlands Park Primary School

INFORMATION

We hope you have enjoyed reading this book - and that you will continue to enjoy it in the coming years.

If you like reading and writing poetry drop us a line, or give us a call, and we'll send you a free information pack.

Write to

        Young Writers Information
        1-2 Wainman Road
        Woodston
        Peterborough
        PE2 7BU